Creative Writing and the Experiences of Others

In times that are rife with complex manifestations of identity politics, writing classrooms across the world are hosting heated debates about what it means for authors to write about experiences outside their own. This book focuses on writing as the act of witnessing when the writers themselves were not present to witness in person. It seeks to answer the questions that come along with these experiences, such as what might it mean to write in order "to watch," "to try and understand," "to never look away," and "to never forget" when the writer is an outsider to an experience? What might it mean to write about others in ways that do not essentialize or sensationalize, and in ways that are as humble, ethical, and responsible as possible? What might it mean to bear witness through the written word while engaged in a constant (re)negotiation with one's own positioning i.e., to cultivate a condition of critical empathy that doesn't also have the consequence of creative paralysis?

Nandita Dinesh is Dean of Academic Administration at Mount Tamalpais College and serves incarcerated students inside San Quentin State Prison.

Routledge Focus on Literature

Supernatural Creatures in Arabic Literary Tradition
Ahmed Al-Rawi

Writing In-between
Collaborative meaning making in performative writing
Nandita Dinesh

Billy Lynn's Long Halftime Walk
Flags, Football, and the NFL's "Foxy" Patriotism Problem
Lisa Ferguson

Bosnian Authors in a European Window
A Comparative Study
Keith Doubt

Contemporary Irish Masculinities
Male Homosociality in Sally Rooney's Novels
Angelos Bollas

Creative Writing and the Experiences of Others
Strategies for Outsiders
Nandita Dinesh

For more information about this series, please visit: www.routledge.com/Routledge-Focus-on-Literature/book-series/RFLT

Creative Writing and the Experiences of Others

Strategies for Outsiders

Nandita Dinesh

NEW YORK AND LONDON

First published 2024
by Routledge
605 Third Avenue, New York, NY 10158

and by Routledge
4 Park Square, Milton Park, Abingdon, Oxon, OX14 4RN

Routledge is an imprint of the Taylor & Francis Group, an informa business

Library of Congress Cataloging-in-Publication Data
Names: Dinesh, Nandita, author.
Title: Creative writing & the experiences of others :
strategies for outsiders / Nandita Dinesh.
Description: New York, NY : Routledge, 2024. |
Series: Routledge focus on literature |
Includes bibliographical references and index. |
Identifiers: LCCN 2023059178 | ISBN 9781032688701 (hardback) |
ISBN 9781032688725 (paperback) | ISBN 9781032688749 (ebook)
Subjects: LCSH: Creative writing. | Authorship–Moral and ethical aspects.
Classification: LCC PN187 .D56 2024 | DDC 808–dc23/eng/20240215
LC record available at https://lccn.loc.gov/2023059178

ISBN: 9781032688701 (hbk)
ISBN: 9781032688725 (pbk)
ISBN: 9781032688749 (ebk)

DOI: 10.4324/9781032688749

Typeset in Times New Roman
by Newgen Publishing UK

Contents

Introduction—Setting the Stage

"To never simplify what is complicated or complicate what is simple [...] to watch. To try and understand. To never look away. And never, never to forget."

(Roy, 1999, p. 102)

My life as a writer started by accident, during a year in which I was travelling constantly, alone, with long-winded existential emails being one of the few ways I had to keep in touch with my people across continents. I remember sitting at Bourbon Coffee in Kigali, in the days when it had first opened in 2007, and tearing up as I was trying to tell my family in Coimbatore and my friends in New York City about what I was experiencing. Sipping my cappuccino in the luxury of a café that only expats like me could afford to frequent, the *thing* inside me started to stir. You know, the *thing*. The *thing* that stirs when you know you're ready to write something. The *thing* that cannot be explained, that is perhaps more powerful in not being explained, that makes the act of writing—and the written word—become something like a burning need. Something you *must* do. Something you *need* to get out through your fingers because it needs to come out. The thing that I'm feeling as I write this sitting in a curb-side café in San Francisco almost fifteen years later.

I started writing to share *my* stories. To talk about what I was seeing and smelling and feeling and hearing...but somewhere along the way, in ways that I cannot remember, writing became something else. It became about engaging with the world. It became about politics. About ethics. About solidarity. About ally-ship, witness,

DOI: 10.4324/9781032688749-1

responsibility. Somehow, in ways that I cannot fully articulate, writing became—and still is—about understanding lives that are different from my own.

In times that are rife with complex manifestations of identity politics, writing classrooms across the world are hosting heated debates about what it means for authors to write about experiences outside their own. Some say an unequivocal "no": writers should *not* create from or about circumstances that we have not experienced ourselves. Others are convinced that the art of writing will wither into decay if authors don't have permission to give voice to the lives of others. A few believe that it is power and positioning that are deciding factors: writers who represent groups that have contextual privilege need to be more wary—because of legacies of misrepresentation, appropriation, and over-simplification—when writing about others who have less power. And amidst the many combinations and permutations of these opinions, there are those like me: authors for whom writing about non-lived experiences, about others' lives, is a way of witnessing; of embodying responsible citizenship in a world that we are lucky enough to experience through relative comfort. So, how do we do it? How do we do this work of writing about others' lives as ethically, responsibly, humbly, and respectfully as possible? This is the question that has consumed my work as a writer, educator, and researcher for almost two decades.

Through this book, I want to share with you—someone I imagine to be a writer with similar hopes for your craft—seven strategies that have taken me multiple trials and errors to be able to articulate. Strategies that continue to evolve in each of my writing projects and that are shared in this book via three sections:

Section One

In the first section, *Examine*, you will see the text for a screenplay titled *The Trials.* Interspersed between the scenes, you will find boxes that invite you to examine a particular strategy and its manifestation in the creative text. A work of fiction that I started writing when I first moved to San Francisco, *The Trials* emerged when I encountered in the streets of these United States—for the first time in almost a decade of living in different parts of this country—a kind of inequality that I had only otherwise experienced in my other home, India; encounters that also coincided with the time Russia began its invasion of Ukraine.

So, I wrote. I wrote *The Trials* to try and respond, the only way I knew how, to the conflicts that existed in spheres both personal and political.

Section Two

Each part of the second section, *Explore*, begins with an invitation for how you might explore the three texts that follow while using the strategies that you examined in Section One and *The Trials*. Each of the three texts in Section Two's seven parts is a news story from Global Voices, a publication that generously allows open access to, and free adaption of, the articles on its platform. Not knowing who you are and to which places or contexts you might be insiders or outsiders, I have chosen to showcase (lightly edited) versions of stories from the last three years, 2021–2023, that span a diversity of contexts, a range of socio-political events, and a multitude of lived experiences.

If the invitation that precedes each of the seven parts of Section Two, each containing three Global Voices texts, is insufficient direction for you to be able to kickstart your exploration, you will see guidance following each article entitled *NOT SURE WHERE TO START?* The starting points that are offered in these spaces are simply that: starting points. I hope that they will help unlock your creativity and your own way of exploring the strategy in question.

Section Three

The final section will invite you to experiment with the seven strategies that are examined via *The Trials* in Section One and explored through the news articles in Section Two. While there is guidance provided in this section for how you might want to structure your experiments, you are welcome to use writing projects that you are already working on as points of departure instead. Throughout the first section's directed examination, to the second section's guided exploration, to the final section's self-directed experimentation, we will return to these questions:

- How might we (outsiders) write about others' lives in ways that do not essentialize or sensationalize; ways that are as ethical and responsible and humble and respectful as possible?
- How might we enrich and expand our understanding of what it means "to watch. To try and understand. To never look away. And

never, never to forget" when we—the witnesses, the writers—are outsiders to an experience?

Before heading into the sections, although I end the book with these very words, I would be remiss to not begin with them too:

Despite your best efforts to integrate the strategies outlined in this book, your past, present, or future endeavours to devise new ones, and your earnest attempts to write about experiences to which you are an outsider, there will always be some experiences and contexts and phenomena that you—with the particular kinds of "outsider-ness" that you bring—should step away from. Precisely to be ethical, responsible, humble, and respectful.

Listen to your internal compass.

Be honest.

Some stories might never be yours to tell.

And that's okay.

Work Cited

Roy, A (1999). *The Cost of Living*. New York: Modern Library.

Section One

Examine *The Trials*

As you go through this section, use the QR code or the footnoted link to visit the online forum for this book and share thoughts or questions from your examinations.[1]

1 https://nanditadinesh.com/creative-writing-and-the-experiences-of-others

DOI: 10.4324/9781032688749-2

SCENE ONE: INT. A ROOM

CANDIDATE #1 and CANDIDATE #2 are seated across from each other. Their task: to look into each other's eyes, without looking away, for one minute.

An on-screen timer counts down from 60 to 0.

CANDIDATE #1 can't help but avert her eyes every ten seconds or so. She must take a breath and refocus before she can look back into CANDIDATE #2's eyes again.

CANDIDATE #2 is dishevelled, quite the contrast in his appearance to the very put-together demeanour of CANDIDATE #1. Every time the woman sitting across from him averts her eyes, he shifts in his chair, just a little bit.

Although CANDIDATE #2's body shows his awareness of CANDIDATE #1's averted gaze, he does not look away from her. He cannot look away from her. His simultaneous discomfort and confidence create an odd duality. It is as though CANDIDATE #2 knows why CANDIDATE #1 is looking away from him and wants to make sure that she knows; that she knows that he knows. That she knows that he knows she is uncomfortable because she is sitting across from someone whom she has been taught—all her life—to look away from.

WHEN THE TIMER HITS 0, CUT TO:

SCENE TWO: INT. A CAFÉ

CANDIDATE #1 sits across from TEAM MEMBER #1 and TEAM MEMBER #2.

CANDIDATE #1
What is it supposed to accomplish?

TEAM MEMBER #1
Well, it's… what this iteration of the Trial is meant to explore
is whether a certain number of minutes of unbroken eye contact

between two people—we're starting with four minutes because of the results we obtained from the last round—umm… so the hypothesis of this iteration of the Trial is to test if, even between strangers… if… ummm… if four minutes of this kind of uninterrupted gazing can increase a sense of connection. Intimacy.

CANDIDATE #1
Intimacy?

TEAM MEMBER #2
Maybe that's not entirely the right word, but the general idea—the hope, rather—is that this kind of exercise might help create a bond between strangers. Between people who, otherwise… who otherwise are unlikely to know each other… to meet each other. You know? Because they tend to occupy different… you know, in the real world, these two people are unlikely to have much reason to interact with each other. We're intentionally choosing s who fit those criteria. So, essentially—

CANDIDATE #1
You're trying to figure out how this shared moment can… might… create some kind of connection.

TEAM MEMBER #1

Right.

(pause)

CANDIDATE #1
A connection that lasts like… you're hoping that the two Candidates will become… I don't know… friends…? Or… I don't know… what kind of connection are you trying to create? Or can you not tell me that?

TEAM MEMBER #1
Well, to be honest, we don't know. You and—well, if you agree to participate, you and your partner for the Trial will be the first two Candidates to try the four-minute time limit. So, we don't really know what kind of connection you might… you know… because

we've never really tried this particular set of conditions before. Does that make sense?

CANDIDATE #1
Yes... yeah... I think I understand. Can you tell me who you are likely to pair me with?

TEAM MEMBER #2
Unfortunately, we can't reveal that information. It's actually not our choice. There's another team working on picking the other person... and neither of us has information about the other—we don't know who they're picking; they don't know who we're picking. We only share that information once our respective Candidates have confirmed their participation.

TEAM MEMBER #1
Also, just to clarify: this process of anonymity was also something that was designed as an experimental condition based on responses from the last iteration of the Trial.
(pause)

CANDIDATE #1
Have the results been published yet?

TEAM MEMBER #1
From the last iteration of the Trial?

CANDIDATE #1
Yeah... I know there was a push at one point to make the results and analysis available within one week of each iteration's end. Is that still the case?

TEAM MEMBER #2
So, that's actually something that has changed quite significantly over the years. We found that this one-week turnaround severely limited our Candidate pool for the next iteration because the people who had read the report, came in with... you know—

CANDIDATE #1
Preconceived notions about how they should behave.

TEAM MEMBER #2
Exactly.
CANDIDATE #1
Yeah. No, I can understand that.
You know, when I first moved here, I was obsessed with the
Trials. Literally, OBSESSED… There's nothing like this where
I grew up and I was—I am still—fascinated by what you all are
trying to do. But then life happened… and I haven't been able
to be as involved as I would have liked to be… All this to say, in
theory, I am really interested in collaborating with you, but I must
ask… Why me? I'm just curious, you know… there must be so
many people who are on your database… the Trials are quite… you
know… it's something many people would like to be part of.

TEAM MEMBER #1
Yes… we have about 10,000 people on the database at the
moment.

CANDIDATE #1
Exactly. So, why me?

CUT TO:

Examine Scenes One and Two: Allegories and Abstractions

In your imagination, in which part of the world do the previous two scenes happen? When you imagine Candidate #2, how do you imagine him: his height; his build; his likeness? What about Candidate #1: how do you imagine her? Why do you think she is averting her eyes from the person across from her? And the team that's conducting the Trials: where do you imagine them to be?

When you do not have any contextual guideposts that help you situate the place or the people in a piece of writing, what do you draw from?

What is lost, or gained, by leaving so much about the context open to the imagination of an audience—be it a reader or viewer?

What if the first scene had been written like this instead?

INT. A ROOM IN THE BASEMENT OF THE TRIALS HEADQUARTERS ON GEARY BOULEVARD

David and Asmita are seated across from each other. Their task: to look into each other's eyes, without looking away, for one minute.

An on-screen timer counts down from 60 to 0.

Asmita can't help but avert her eyes every ten seconds or so. She must take a breath and refocus before she can look back into David's eyes again. She wears Lulu lemon slacks, a non-descript T-shirt, a Patagonia vest, and purple and pink Hoka One Ones.

David is dishevelled; his worldly possessions lie in a rolling cart that's beside him. He wears a threadbare coat, somewhere between brown and green; pants that once used to be khaki, with a tear running down its right leg; his pants sit low and there's a sliver of chequered boxers that can be seen above them. He's wearing Hoka One Ones too, shoes he acquired years ago; he needs a new pair. He carries all the markers that lead Asmita to believe that he is a person experiencing homelessness: his hair is matted and looks like it hasn't been brushed or washed in a while; he is unshaven; streaks of what could be dirt or severe sunburn line his face. More than anything else, what Asmita can't seem to stop looking at is the way the fingers on his right hand are picking at the skin on the palm of his left. A particular "tic," if one can call it that, which Asmita has learned to expect from anyone using fentanyl.

Although David seems to be aware of Asmita's judgements and her inability to stop herself from looking at his fingers, he does not look away from her. David's simultaneous discomfort and confidence create an odd duality. It's like David knows why Asmita is looking away from him—like he knows how she is looking at him—and wants to make sure that she knows; that she knows that he knows. That she knows that he knows that she is uncomfortable because she is sitting across from someone whom she has been taught—all her life—to look away from.

WHEN THE TIMER HITS 0, CUT TO:

What does this new version of the scene do, or not, as compared to the first version that does not name the place or the characters?

Given the explicitly mentioned theme of this book, i.e. to explore what more ethical modes of representing others might be, why do you think I might have chosen the strategy of the general rather than the specific, the anonymous rather than the named?

To be clear, I do not think there is a one-size-fits-all approach for how specifically a setting should (not) be constructed. I have written works where it seemed more ethical and more responsible to be extremely specific in establishing the characters and their worlds. I have written others where it seemed more ethical, and more responsible to adopt an approach that is like the "context-less-ness" of this screenplay. Here are the guideposts that I use in my decision-making:

- **Intention:** If I intend to generate discussion about the human complexities of what is happening in a particular context of conflict, will being hyper-specific about the setting be more likely to result in controversial debates about whose "side" the writing takes, rather than being about the larger conditions of war? If yes, if I'm trying to provoke broad-based reflection rather than place-specific debate, I am likely to choose *less* specificity in the work's setting.

- **Time**: Have I spent enough time in the contexts that I am describing—not through archival research or in my imagination, but in the real world—to make my written attempts to characterize these places and peoples nuanced and complex? If the answer is no, I tend to choose a generic, allegorized approach like *The Trials* rather than adopting an error-ridden specificity.
- **Partnership:** Do I know someone from the specific context or community that I am writing about? If I don't know a single person who will give me honest criticism about my portrayals of a setting and the characters I'm placing within it, I prefer crafting semi-fictional settings rather than deploying real-world ones.

SCENE THREE: TO CAMERA

TEAM LEADER
This only works if you do it with me.

I want you to focus on my eyes.

Just look at my eyes. Into my eyes. And focus on them.

That's it.

Wherever you're sitting or standing, just look into my eyes.

We'll try it for thirty seconds.

(A timer counts down from 30 to 0.)

WHEN THE TIMER HITS 0, CUT TO:

SCENE FOUR: INT. A CLASSROOM

A group of ten TEAM MEMBERS and a TEAM LEADER are seated around a table.

The TEAM MEMBERs are an intentionally diverse team: in terms of gender, race, socio-economic status, and everything else. The only area in which they are not so diverse is linguistically. They all speak and understand English.

However, English doesn't have to be the first language of all the people in the room. They are welcome to speak in accents. Dialects. Versions of English that lie somewhere between dialects and different languages.

As TEAM MEMBERs #1 and #2 speak about their choice of candidate, their descriptions are accompanied by IMAGES that complement what they verbalize. How the IMAGES appear, disappear, or transition is at the discretion of the director—the more otherworldly the IMAGES, the better.

IMAGE: FACE OF CANDIDATE #1

TEAM MEMBER #2
She's not from here. She moved here, ummm… she moved here about ten years ago. And since then, she has been teaching in several different schools—

TEAM MEMBER #1
High schools mostly—
IMAGE: CANDIDATE #1 WORKING WITH STUDENTS

TEAM MEMBER #2
Right, exactly. Actually, before we go there, we should rewind a bit and tell you about our para—

TEAM MEMBER #1
Right, we should tell you why we chose her—

TEAM MEMBER #2
Would you like to do the honours?

TEAM MEMBER #1
No, please, go ahead.

TEAM MEMBER #2
You sure?
(TEAM MEMBER #1 nods affirmatively.)

IMAGE: DIFFERENT PICTURE OF CANDIDATE #1
WORKING WITH STUDENTS

TEAM MEMBER #2
Ok, so for our member of the Candidate pair, we both decided from the beginning that we wanted to pick an educator as one of our Candidates With More Privilege.

TEAM MEMBER #1
We thought it would be… since we want to increase the odds of long-term connections, we thought… you know—

TEAM MEMBER #2
Right, who better than an educator to… like, if the Trial affects an educator, there is the possibility for them to… you know… in a tangible way, to share what they have learned and discovered with their students. They are already part of an environment that is centred on learning so maybe the school can get involved in sustaining the relationship between our Candidate and the person they encounter. You know, we both felt like an educator would be the kind of Candidate With More Privilege who could be able to, you know… like… what am I trying to say…

IMAGE: CANDIDATE #1 WORKING WITH COLLEAGUES

TEAM MEMBER #1
Like they could build, based on their experience of the Trial, you know, they could—

TEAM LEADER
Slow down, both of you. There's no need to rush through this. Take a breath. We're not going anywhere.

TEAM MEMBER #1
Right. Sorry. We're just nervous and excited.

TEAM MEMBER #2
Yeah. We felt like we had cracked something… with this educator angle and… we just wanted to…
(takes a breath)

Anyway.

IMAGE: CANDIDATE #1 PRESENTING AT A CONFERENCE

TEAM MEMBER #2 (CONT'D)
We wanted to choose an educator as the partner for our part
of the pairing because of the long-term outcomes that might be
possible regardless of whoever they have chosen as the other
Candidate.
(Gestures to TEAM MEMBER #3 and TEAM MEMBER #4.)

TEAM LEADER
Okay, great. I think that part is clear. You wanted to choose
someone who has the kind of work that would naturally allow for
longer-term connections to happen if the Candidate is affected in
this way. Great. I think that's a very sensible approach... other
than the fact that she is an educator is there anything else that
made you—

TEAM MEMBER #2
Right, yes, I meant to—sorry, I didn't mean to interrupt
you. Sorry.

IMAGE: CANDIDATE #1's DATABASE PROFILE PAGE

TEAM LEADER
It's ok. Go on. What else about this participant made you think
that they would be a good Candidate for the Trial?

TEAM MEMBER #1
She's not... you know... she's well off. She's elegant and refined.
She's sophisticated. Not like... you know... Not—

IMAGE: CANDIDATE #1 DECKED UP AT A CEREMONY
OF SOME KIND

TEAM MEMBER #6
—the stereotype of an immigrant?

TEAM MEMBER #1
That's not—

TEAM MEMBER #2
Yeah, exactly—
(awkward laughter)

TEAM MEMBER #1
It sounds wrong when you put it like that but you're right... she's
an interesting Candidate because when... you know, when we were
first tasked with choosing the Candidate With More Privilege, we
both found ourselves thinking of a particular type of person. Not
someone like her... but when we saw her profile in the database...
she fitted so many of those boxes of privilege that we had defined as
being... you know... that we had defined as being part of the profile
of the kind of person we were tasked with choosing and... can you
take over? I feel like I'm being really unclear.
(laughs nervously)

IMAGE: CANDIDATE #1 WITH HER FAMILY

TEAM MEMBER #2
You're being clear, but sure, I can just wrap up. When we came
across this Candidate's profile, we were both really surprised that
she met many of the markers of privilege we had articulated: socio-
economic status; sexual orientation... but yet, she did not... like...
she didn't embody all the identity markers of the kind of person that
we had first assumed we'd end up choosing—based on race and
gender, for example. And immigration status. So, that... "surprise"
factor... that she lives many of the privileges that would give her
relative status in our society and yet, is also characterized by being
less privileged than others... it was this sort of... complex combin-
ation of factors, in addition to the fact that she's an educator, that
really seemed to bring a certain... sort of... beautiful unexpected-
ness. Does that make sense? It wasn't as reductive as saying "Hey,
she's not the stereotypical immigrant," but it would also be disin-
genuous to say that that wasn't part of the reason we think she will
be an intriguing Candidate.

TEAM MEMBER #1

Right. This is not the predictable Candidate With More Privilege
and we thought it would make for a more creative... complex
contribution.

(pause)

IMAGE: COLLAGE OF ALL THE IMAGES PRESENTED
OF CANDIDATE #1

TEAM MEMBER #3

I think it's wonderful that you both decided to approach your
choice of Candidate in this way because we were grappling with the
same kind of thing when we were choosing our Candidate With Less
Privilege. We wanted to choose someone who would bring more...
complexity to the Trials.

IMAGE: FACE OF CANDIDATE #2

CUT TO:

Examine Scenes Three and Four: Autoethnography

Autoethnography, in simple terms, is a constant recognition
of—and reckoning with—the very specific lenses through
which the individual who is performing a response, analysis,
or interpretation engages with their subject(s). An approach that
aims to highlight the inevitable subjectivity when observing
or engaging with others, it is a framework that I use in a few
different ways when I seek to engage with life experiences that
are not my own.

In *The Trials*, for example, the entire framework of the screenplay might be seen as autoethnographic in nature. When thinking
about how to write a piece around homelessness in San Francisco,
the only way I could think to ethically approach the subject—as
someone who has never had to experience life unhoused, as an
educator, as a privileged immigrant—was to create a container
that would capture the intellectual detachment that underscores
my engagement. I chose an explicitly research-based world
where it is precisely people who *don't* have a lived experience

who are trying (and failing and trying again) to understand complicated social and political dynamics that they are outsiders to. By choosing a container that reflects the detached lens of my "outsider-ness," I want to constantly remind the reader that this written exploration is nothing more nor less than an attempt that is made by a very particular kind of observer.

In addition to the larger frame of the world of *The Trials*, I crafted the character of Candidate #1 to reflect aspects of my own identity and positioning: someone with privilege who also fits within a larger social and political category (of the immigrant) that is often understood as being without the kind of access that I have. Now, no one who doesn't know me could likely tell whether the abovementioned choices are autoethnographic or simply creative. Where this type of autoethnographic approach is central to me, however, is in navigating my internal debates on my right to engage with experiences outside my own.

There are two different ways in which I have explored the use of autoethnography in my writing:

- Implicit autoethnography: An approach in which methods and strategies of autoethnography are woven into the world of the creative response—as setting, as character, as plot—in such a way that it is only those familiar with the author who are likely to notice the presence of this methodology. The Trials is an example of how this might manifest.
- Explicit autoethnography: Strategies that centre the voice of the outsider-author in ways that make it obvious to any reader the particular identity and positioning from which the non-lived experience is being addressed. Chronicles from Kashmir (Dinesh, 2020) is an example of how I've used explicit autoethnography in my writing.

Later in the book, in the *Explore* section, you will be invited to engage with obvious and explicit modes of autoethnography, rather than an embedded and implicit approach like *The Trials*.

Work Cited

Dinesh. N. (2020). *Chronicles from Kashmir: An Annotated, Multimedia Script.* Cambridge: Open Book Publishers.

SCENE FIVE: EXT. A STREET

The street and its sidewalks have been transformed into an event with multiple stalls, the kind of event that offers free services to people living on the streets of the city: legal aid, haircuts, showers, massages, and health services. CANDIDATE #2 has just stepped out of a trailer that doubles as a shower; he is having a cup of coffee. TEAM MEMBER #3 is seated beside him. TEAM MEMBER #4 is having a seemingly serious conversation on their phone.

CANDIDATE #2
Those Trials are still going on?

TEAM MEMBER #3
Yes, sir. We've learned a lot from the past iterations, and this is an updated... you know, it's a new approach based on what we've learned. New experimental conditions that we are testing.
(pause)

CANDIDATE #2
I signed up under very different circumstances.

TEAM MEMBER #3
Oh. I'm so sorry. If you'd rather not be part of the Trial database anymore, I can contact—

CANDIDATE #2
No, it's fine. I'm still interested in the whole... thing. I'm just saying... when I signed up on the database, I was a student in graduate school. Life has... life has taken a few turns since then. I just didn't think to take myself off the database. I'm amazed you even found me.

TEAM MEMBER #3
We have a very good logistics team. If you don't mind my asking: what were you studying? When you were in graduate school?

CANDIDATE #2
Your partner seems to be having a very serious conversation over there.

TEAM MEMBER #3

Oh, sorry. He's just—I'm sure he's dealing with an emergency otherwise he would definitely be payi—sorry about that.
(TEAM MEMBER #3 tries to get TEAM MEMBER #4's attention, to no avail.)

You were saying—

CANDIDATE #2

Yeah, where were we... what was I studying? That's what you asked me. Architecture.

TEAM MEMBER #3

Architecture.

CANDIDATE #2

Didn't expect that?

TEAM MEMBER #3

No! Yes—I mean. Sorry. To be honest, I didn't know what to expect. It's my first time at... you know... an event like this. I... We... ummm... yeah. We didn't know what to expect. Especially if you'd still be open to even speaking with us.
(CANDIDATE #2 and TEAM MEMBER #3 drink their coffee in silence.)

CANDIDATE #2

How long have you been part of this... whole Trial thing?

TEAM MEMBER #3

I'm quite new to the programme, actually. I just enlisted about three months ago... this is my first assignment... after the orientation and everything. It's just something I've always wanted to do. Be part of building the Trials... well, not building them per se, but developing them. Evolving them somehow.

CANDIDATE #2

Why?

TEAM MEMBER #3
Why did I want to join? My family… it's just something that everyone has done from, like, my great-grandmother down to me. It's what was… you know…

CANDIDATE #2
Expected.

TEAM MEMBER #3
Something like that… expected, but also a choice. I really do believe in the mission of the Trials. Of what everyone involved in it… what we're hoping to create in the world.

CANDIDATE #2
And what's that?

TEAM MEMBER #3
You know… the mission to work toward a world that is more… equitable. More empathetic. More just… A mission to understand how to make humans care about each other. Especially the kinds of humans who would never meet each other in the real world and yet those who… if they could meet under the right conditions, might be exactly the kind of connections that are needed to change everyone's lives for the better… I know it probably sounds pretentious to be talking about all these… like… you know… these lofty intangibles when—

CANDIDATE #2
When we are where we are.
(They both drink their coffee.)

CANDIDATE #2 (CONT'D)
Why me?

TEAM MEMBER #3
In your database profile… you were very open about your childhood and the things that… it was clear that you had fought to get where you are—were—at the time and that you… you know… had experienced… you know…

CANDIDATE #2
A lot of shit.

TEAM MEMBER #3
Right.

CANDIDATE #2 (smiles)
So, you saw my entry and said "Hey, there's a guy who lived through a lot of shit, let's get him involved in the Trial"?

TEAM MEMBER #3
Something like that… you're the kind of Candidate that we were asked to invite to be part of the Trial. A person who has had a lot of… you know… life experience. The kind that many others don't.

CANDIDATE #2 (smiles)
Look around you. There are many who do. I still would like to know how your team found me.

TEAM MEMBER #3
I can give you the contact information for someone in that department. I'm sure they will tell you how they were able to find your location.

CANDIDATE #2
I'm sure they contacted my parents. I think it was their information that I remember listing on the database profile thing…

TEAM MEMBER #3
I… if this doesn't feel like the right thing for you to do… I'm really sorry if we overstepped in trying to find you. I can te—

CANDIDATE #2
Nothing to apologize for. I'm just… you know, I never know where a day is going to go but this… this is all very unexpected. That's all. Give me some time to think about it? Can you come back here next week? Same time?

CUT TO:

SCENE SIX: INT. A CAR

TEAM MEMBER #3 and TEAM MEMBER #4 are leaving the event on the street.

TEAM MEMBER #4
Look, I said I'm sorry.

TEAM MEMBER #3
It was so fucking offensive, man.

TEAM MEMBER #4
I had to take the call.

TEAM MEMBER #3
Really? It was a life-or-death situation? It was so fucking disrespectful to him. It'll be a wonder if he agrees to work with us after the way you—

TEAM MEMBER #4
You've made your point, okay?
(silence)

TEAM MEMBER #3
Why did you even sign up for the course if you care so little about it? Maybe the rumours are right.

TEAM MEMBER #4
What rumours?

TEAM MEMBER #3
That you were made to sign up for community service hours. That you didn't choose to be here voluntarily.

TEAM MEMBER #4
Wow. That's the rumour, huh?
(silence)

TEAM MEMBER #3
I don't think you should present with me.

TEAM MEMBER #4
What?

TEAM MEMBER #3
I don't think you should present with me. To the class. You've
barely done anything.

You were on the phone when we were supposed to be articulating
the parameters for Candidate selection. And now again when we
were supposed to be inviting him together. You just... just... I'm
going to ask if I can complete the rest of the project solo.
(long silence)

TEAM MEMBER #4
You realize the irony, right?
(silence)

This whole thing is about empathy. Locating empathy. Finding a
way to connect with people who are radically different from what we
know... and all you're doing is assuming the worst about me without...
(pause)

TEAM MEMBER #3
Without what?

TEAM MEMBER #4
Without trying to see where I might be coming from. Why I
might be acting this way. What might be causing my
seeming disinterest.
Maybe we should stare into each other's eyes for four minutes.
(silence)

TEAM MEMBER #3
You're right. I'm sorry. I should have talked to you about it the
first time and tried to—I'm sorry. This is just... I need to do well on
the team. I need to... I want to be invited back. I want to be part of
the Trial leadership someday and... I need this to go well.
But you're right. If I end up forgetting the first principles of the
whole thing in the process, it's not going to matter.
(long silence)

TEAM MEMBER #4
My brother died last month. His insurance pay-outs are just
starting to be processed now and his wife... she's the one who has
been calling me. There's so much paperwork and part of it must be
filled with information from me and our parents...
the filing deadline is coming up.
(silence)

TEAM MEMBER #3
I'm so sorry.

TEAM MEMBER #4
I should have said something earlier. My mind is... I'm all over
the place. I should have told the Team Leader when I was allocated
to pick a Candidate... it would have been better for me to do this
another ti—what are you doing? Dude!
(TEAM MEMBER #3 makes a sharp U-turn)

TEAM MEMBER #3
We're going back so that you can introduce yourself to our
Candidate and extend your invitation.

TEAM MEMBER #4
He's not going to be there still!

TEAM MEMBER #3
If he isn't, he isn't. But we're going to try.
(silence)

TEAM MEMBER #4
Thank you.

TEAM MEMBER #3
Sorry I was such an ass.

CUT TO:

Examine Scenes Five and Six: Lack of Understanding

I want to draw your attention to the use of *silences* and *pauses* in the preceding scenes and the types of emotional distance they might capture between characters.

It is sometimes instinctual for an outsider who is unaware of the sheer number of layers to a lived experience outside of their own to make things explainable, understandable, or articulable. Whereas the potential of our positioning as outsiders might arise more poignantly in the things that *cannot* be understood. In *The Trials,* these gaps in understanding are captured through pauses and silences, through misunderstandings that are made explicit in dialogue.

Examine the scene that came before and identify some moments that, in your opinion, display the characters' *lack* of understanding with or for each other. How would those moments have shifted if there had been more certainty in the characters words and actions, for example if CANDIDATE #2 did not display any scepticism of the Trials, or if the TEAM MEMBERS extended each other an idealized understanding from the start. What might textual representations of *mis*understanding— through dialogue and pauses and silences—allow an outsider-writer to capture about their own ignorance?

As you consider the lack of understanding between you and the settings and people in your writing, here are a few types of gaps to consider:

What are the gaps in your socio-political or historical knowledge? What resources have informed your existing knowledge about a place, people, or condition and what biases might your sources be shaped by? What bias guides your search for information?

What are the gaps in your encounters with the others in your writing? Is your exploration only imaginative? Is it based only on archival research? Have you been able to engage, personally, in the real world, with some or many of the stakeholder groups that are involved in the situation you are writing about?

What are the cultural gaps? What might be the gestures and habits and customs that are unfamiliar to you? What are everyday practices and processes that you take for granted? What are you imposing on an understanding of others that is informed by the hegemonies that pervade your own thinking and existence?

How do the nexuses between these different types of gaps manifest in a distance that is unique between each outsider-writer and the contexts they seek to write about? More importantly, how might we capture such distances in our writing to *humbly* share the borders of our understanding and in so doing, mitigate any possible readerly misconception that we might be offering an expertise that we do not have?

SCENE SEVEN: INT. A ROOM

CANDIDATE #1 and CANDIDATE #2 are seated across from each other. They look into each other's eyes for one minute—a timer counts down from 60 seconds.

They are both smiling, apparently extremely comfortable with looking into each other's eyes now.

Slowly, their smiles become more poignant, more intense, until both their eyes fill up with tears.

A tear rolls down one person's cheek; the other's hand seems to want to move to wipe it off. But that impulse is controlled.

WHEN THE TIMER HITS 0, CUT TO:

SCENE EIGHT: INT. A CAFÉ

Debrief interview between TEAM MEMBER #1, TEAM MEMBER #2, and CANDIDATE #1.

CANDIDATE #1

I didn't think it would… I mean, I didn't know what to expect so… I can't say that I didn't think this would happen… but the intensity of looking into his eyes and of… especially at some point when both of us had tears in our eyes… it was like… I don't know how to describe it. It's like I was in that moment but also outside of it, in some way… watching myself from outside my body and marvelling at this curious experience that made me emotional in ways that… yeah… in ways that I didn't know were… possible, I suppose.

TEAM MEMBER #1

Is this the first time you've had that kind of connection with someone who… you know…

CANDIDATE #1
It's the first time I've had any kind of connection to anyone like
him. At home...

VISUAL: THROUGHOUT CANDIDATE #1'S NARRATIVES
OF HOME (BELOW), WE SEE IMAGES FROM HER YOUTH.
WHILE SOME ALLUSIONS TO REAL-WORLD CONTEXTS ARE
WELCOME—IN THIS WRITER'S IMAGINATION, CANDIDATE
#1 GREW UP IN INDIA—WHAT'S SHOWN ON SCREEN NEED
NOT BE IDENTIFIABLE AS BEING A SPECIFIC COUNTRY.

JUST AS THE CONTENT IS OPEN TO THE DIRECTORIAL
IMAGINATION, SO IS THE FORM: THE VISUALS CAN BE
SHOWN AS FLASHBACKS WITH VOICEOVER; THEY COULD
JUST AS WELL BE ENVISIONED AS A SPLIT SCREEN, I.E.
HALF THE SCREEN CONTAINS THE IMAGES, WHILE THE
OTHER HALF CONTAINS THE IMAGE OF CANDIDATE #1,
SPEAKING.

CANDIDATE #1 (CONT'D)
Where I grew up, people living on the streets are everywhere...
people who can't afford a meal... or a home or food... it's something
that I just... it was normal, you know? I'm not saying that it—that
approach—was right or anything like that... I know how problematic
all that sounds but... that's how it was.

Somehow, growing up surrounded by that kind of... thing...
I think I just... I know this sounds bad, but I think I just... like...
got used to it. It was just something that happened. Something that
still happens. Some people live this way and you just... you get on
with your life, you know? Or at least, that's what I did... what I still
do when I go back to visit... I see people living on the streets and
I just... you know... look away... or look at them and think "Man,
that's heartbreaking but there's nothing I can do about it, so I'm just
not going to think about it too much."

I think that's what I did when I came here too. Just... I mean
I noticed them more—the people living on the streets here—I noticed
them more than I notice people on the streets at home... but that's
only because I never expected this kind of... I never expected to see

this here. Somehow, in everything I've heard about this country, it sounded like it was more... you know... I always assumed that this country had somehow figured out how to ensure everyone had a roof over their heads. It just...

I thought these were things that only happened *there*. Not *here*. I... when I finally arrived here and saw so many people on the streets, I just noticed it more. At least in the first month or two, because of how unexpected it all was... I was more sensitive to the presence of this... this phenomenon. Even here though... after a few months had passed, I think it's that ingrained training I've had since my childhood, you know... I know it sounds like an excuse but I just... I just don't register these people as... I mean I know they are people. I know they're human. It's not like I don't know they are human beings... it's just... it's like there's a wall.

The person living on the street and me... we might be inhabiting the same space, the same block even, but there's this transparent but impermeable wall between us... that neither of us can go through. Sorry, that was a long-winded way of... I hope I answered your question?

TEAM MEMBER #1
Yes. Absolutely. You know, we didn't want to mention this to you when we first invited you, because we weren't sure then of who the Candidate across from you would be... but we did wonder if where you grew up—and the differences you encountered when you came here—if that would play a role in how you were able to engage with the person sitting with you...
(pause)

CANDIDATE #1
Are all your pairs like this? One person who is not from here and someone who is... I don't know... not the mainstream image of someone who is from here?

TEAM MEMBER #1
Well, we can disclose this now, but we were tasked with choosing a Candidate With More Privilege—the other team were asked to pick a Candidate With Less Privilege. That's all the instruction they

gave us and we… you know… independent of each other, our two teams defined our parameters for who we thought would be fit for the Trials…

CANDIDATE #1
Candidate With More and Less Privilege… I like that… I've always been frustrated when people talk about immigrants as if we're all… as if we experience the same kinds of suffering… as if we all begin at the same starting line. Some of us… some of us have never really had to want for much. At least, speaking for myself… I've never had to want for anything. I've had so many doors opened to me. So many opportunities that many, even citizens here, cannot access… so… I appreciate that you went with a less conventional choice. Do you think you've inspired similar ideas in the people who will choose Candidates after you?

TEAM MEMBER #1
We don't know yet, actually. Our debrief will happen in a few days and based on the data we've gathered from the Trial, and from these conversations—our peers are talking to the other Candidate as well to hear his thoughts—so based on all of that, we'll discuss with the team whether… you know… we'll stick to the same process or if, you know, the two of you have given us a reason to pursue a different path.
(pause)

TEAM MEMBER #2
You know… you mentioned earlier that you see this "transparent and impermeable wall" between you and… and people who live on the street. And it's such a striking description… I was wondering if we could return to that for a minute and… you know, I know it's only been a week since the Trial and it's not enough time to really… but have you noticed yourself being… different? In how you see that wall… or understand it?
(silence)

CANDIDATE #1
I don't know… don't get me wrong, it's not like I've not been thinking about it. I have. A lot, actually. I've been paying attention to how I behave. How I think. How I act.

VISUAL: THROUGHOUT THE DIALOGUE BELOW, WE SEE IMAGES FROM CANDIDATE #2'S CURRENT CONTEXT, OF PEOPLE WHO HAVE HAD TO MAKE THE STREETS THEIR SHELTERS. WHILE SOME ALLUSIONS TO REAL-WORLD CONTEXTS ARE WELCOME—IN THIS WRITER'S IMAGINATION, THIS CONTEXT IS THE TENDERLOIN IN SAN FRANCISCO—THE PLACE ON SCREEN NEED NOT BE IDENTIFIABLE. JUST AS THE CONTENT IS OPEN TO THE DIRECTORIAL IMAGINATION, SO IS THE FORM: THE VISUALS CAN BE SHOWN AS STILLS WITH VOICEOVER; THEY COULD JUST AS WELL BE ENVISIONED AS A SPLIT SCREEN WITH MOVING IMAGES ON BOTH SIDES.

CANDIDATE #1 (CONT'D)
On the one hand, I know I'm noticing people more. Each time
I see someone living on the street, I look at them and wonder if
maybe it's my partner from the Trial and if it is... you know, if he'd
be comfortable with my approaching him in the real world... so
I guess there's something that's changed... there's something that's
sharper, somehow, in... in how I look and how much I notice... and
just the desire, if I can call it that... the desire to see this person who
I had this short, intense moment with. So that's there, right? That
heightened awareness is there.

But... at the same time, you know, on the other hand, I... I don't
know. It's like the wall became a little more transparent than it was...
like it was actually translucent before... you know... and now it's
become more transparent... but it's still... the wall is still there,
right? It's still impermeable...

I ask myself: if I see my partner from the Trial on the street
tomorrow, will I go up to him and invite him to come have dinner
with me and my family? I don't know... I'd like to think I would, I'd
like to think that I would invite him home and that maybe... maybe
that could even become a regular occurrence and we could... we
could see how things go from there. But then I honestly don't know
if just four minutes of looking into his eyes was enough for me to...
and even if it is enough for me, how is my sister going to respond
to having him... having someone like him—and I know how awful
that sounds as I say that but it's the truth—how would my family...

who have not had even four minutes of connection... who... have their own experiences of the wall and its permeability... how would they respond to someone like him being in our home? I honestly don't know.

CUT TO:

Examine Scenes Seven and Eight: Visual Aesthetics

The Trials is my first screenplay; my only one so far. What does the visual aesthetic of a screenplay offer for the stories being explored, as compared to an approach that looks—on the page, visually—like a more standard essay or story? How can visual aesthetics and experimentation with form become components in a writer's attempts to engage with narratives that fall outside of their own lived experience? Let's take the descriptions of the IMAGES and the monologue that end scene seven and consider their effect with a shift to a different visual aesthetic:

As Candidate #1 speaks, we see images from Candidate #2's current context: of people who have had to make the streets their homes. While some allusions to real-world contexts are welcome—in this writer's imagination, this context is the Tenderloin in San Francisco—the place on screen need not be identifiable. Just as the content is open to the directorial imagination, so is the form: the visuals can be shown as stills with voiceover; they could just as well be envisioned as a split screen with moving images on both sides.

"And on the one hand," Candidate #1 says, "I know I'm noticing people more. Each time I see someone living on the street, I look at them and wonder if maybe it's my partner from the Trial and if it is... you know, if he'd be comfortable with my approaching him in the real world... so, I guess there's something that's changed... there's something that's sharper, somehow, in... in how I look and how much I notice... and just the desire, if I can call it that... the desire to see this person who I had this short intense moment with. So that's there right? [...] I honestly don't know."

To me, experimentation with the visual aesthetic of my texts serves a larger purpose: exploring how the *shape* of the words on the page might communicate my particular kind of "outsiderness" to the content. In the case of *The Trials*, with the presence of a range of different formatting types that are particular to screenplays, I want the fragmentation of the form to visually communicate my own disjointed and incomplete understanding of larger questions surrounding homelessness in San Francisco. I chose *not* to write it as an essay because, to me, a visual aesthetic of flowing paragraphs does not quite perform the jaggedness both of what I see and the many things that I don't.

What kinds of visual aesthetics within writing—how the words look on a page—can capture how a writer might be outside the experiences they write about? And simultaneously, even though they might experiment with the visual aesthetic in their attempt to perform a lack of understanding, how does the writer contend with the risk of alienation, i.e. creating a work that is so beyond the textual shape that the reader is accustomed to, that they find the work to be inaccessible?

Is the potential for inaccessibility a necessary risk that we must take to be more ethical in our representations of lives and experiences that are not our own?

SCENE NINE: INT. A ROOM

CANDIDATE #1 and CANDIDATE #2 are seated across from each other. They look into each other's eyes for one minute—a timer counts down from 60 seconds.

CANDIDATE #1 moves her hand forward, on the tops of her legs, trying to figure out if her partner in the exercise will be willing to receive that type of contact.

Slowly, seeing no reason to question that impulse, CANDIDATE #1's hands keep moving forward until they reach out to the person seated in front of her.

Her hands are immediately met by CANDIDATE #2. And for the time that is remaining, they hold hands.

Smiling.

Their eyes full.

WHEN THE TIMER HITS 0, CUT TO:

SCENE TEN: EXT. THE PORCH OF A BUILDING

CANDIDATE #2 is setting up a temporary shelter for that evening.

CANDIDATE #2
She seemed like a nice person. It was… you know… an experience.

TEAM MEMBER #3   TEAM MEMBER #4

Do you—   Do you—
                                  Go ahead.

TEAM MEMBER #3
Thanks. Ummm… do you think… do you think you might stay in touch with her?

CANDIDATE #2
Stay in touch... I don't know. They gave me her work address—
she works at a school, right?
(TEAM MEMBERS #3 and #4 nod in the affirmative)

Yeah. Schools don't take well to people like me showing up at
their gates unannounced so...let's see if she shows up to the street
event next week. That's the information that I left behind. If she
comes, I'll be there... then we'll see.

TEAM MEMBER #3   TEAM MEMBER #4

What—   What—
You go ahead this time!

TEAM MEMBER #4
Thanks. So, what I was wondering was... you know, I know that
we don't really know if she'll show up next week and what that will
look like... but imagining that she does. Show up at the event next
week, I mean... What would it look like, to you, what would it look
like to stay in touch? What... where could you see the connection
going...?
(silence)

CANDIDATE #2
I don't know.

VISUAL: THROUGHOUT THE DIALOGUE BELOW, WE
SEE IMAGES OF CONFLICTS THAT HAVE HISTORICALLY
OCCURRED BETWEEN INDIVIDUALS THAT HAVE HAD
TO FIND SHELTER ON THE STREETS AND THE HOUSED
INDIVIDUALS THAT SURROUND THEM. WHILE THESE
DEPICTIONS CAN DRAW FROM DOCUMENTED INCIDENCES
IN ANY REAL-WORLD SETTING, THE ON-SCREEN AESTHETIC
MAKES THEM GENERAL IN A WAY THAT DIVORCES THE
IMAGES FROM BEING ABOUT ONE SPECIFIC CONTEXT.

CANDIDATE #2

I have a lot of moving parts in my life already and... it's hard
to think about something like this... I don't know... maybe...
maybe if there was a way for me to get a job or something at her
school, you know... I've always wanted to be involved in education in some way... maybe she could help me get a foot in the
door or something... but... such things. There's a reason they don't
happen.

TEAM MEMBER #4
What do you mean?

CANDIDATE #2

I mean... it's not only one person who can make that kind of
decision is it? She has a boss... her boss has a boss... they all
answer to parents and boards and who knows what else... I can
imagine what a parent would wonder if they got to know that
someone like me was going to be around their children... and
not just parents, there are going to be many people who won't be
comfortable around me because they will... you know... there are
certain tropes about why people who share my living situation
end up where we do. Tropes that are predominantly negative.
And given that, who knows... maybe I understand why they feel
this way.
(silence)

TEAM MEMBER #4

Other than this becoming a working relationship in some way...
is there another path, a future... a long-term... like... connection...
between the two of you... what it can look like?
(pause)

CANDIDATE #2

It would be nice for us to see if we can be friends. If we have
enough in common outside of that... of the Trial... if we have
common interests. Like... if she likes architecture for example... we
could go visit spaces in the city and just get to know each other in
that way, I suppose... the kind of friendship where how I live is just

one aspect of who I am in this moment and… you know, where it
doesn't define how we interact.

I mean… but…. there's a reason these things don't happen.
A reason why you don't see deep, meaningful relationships…
friendships, between people who live on the street and people who
have a secure roof over their heads… There are reasons you don't
see people from these different conditions of home getting together
to just… get coffee. Or watch a movie. The power dynamic… it's
fraught, isn't it? How can two people from these radically diff—
like her and me—how can we be friends without… without the
person who doesn't live on the street becoming obliged to become
some form of… support for their friend? That's… that's a lot of
responsibility.

TEAM MEMBER #3
You don't think there's a way for these two people to define the
kind of relationship where… I don't know… where the person who
might find themselves feeling obliged to do something to change
the conditions of their friend's housing situation… I don't know…
like they control that impulse until if and when their friend asks
for help?

CANDIDATE #2
That's the conundrum, isn't it? Why should I need to ask for help
from someone who is my friend? Shouldn't they be able to learn
what I need and how to help me get it?

I don't know… I'm not sure that even makes sense. Maybe it's
my own… you know… maybe it's my grudge or bias or whatever… against people who don't live like me. Either they're going
to think I'm beyond help… or they're going to think that they need
to keep trying to help me become… help me have a life that's not
this one.

I don't know…

TEAM MEMBER #3
It sounds like you're saying nothing can change.

CANDIDATE #2

Look… if I thought that… I wouldn't have agreed to come to the Trial… I believe that things can happen and change and… whatever… but just because two individual people look each other in the eye for four minutes…? That… I don't know…if change is the goal… that kind of change… I think your Trial has many things to figure out.

CUT TO:

Examine Scenes Nine and Ten: Banalities

Consider the banal action that is at the crux of *The Trials*: two people sitting across from each other, looking into each other's eyes. There is nothing spectacular here, no extraordinary event or condition under which the two Candidates meet, no dramatic setting under which the Team Members evaluate their study. It is all quite ordinary.

Consider what might have been different had the banal been replaced by something more ostensibly dramatic: a dystopian world, for example, or an encounter between the Candidates in an encampment that is being dismantled, or a romantic connection that makes the two protagonists fall in love with each other.

To what extent can focus on the relatively banal mitigate the risk of over-sensationalizing experiences that are not ours? How can quotidian acts—like two people looking at each other—make an outsider-writer *less* susceptible to the stereotypes that might pervade the imagination, with or without their awareness?

In addition to the use of ordinary, simple actions as in *The Trials*, I have also invoked the banal through generally ubiquitous events in human lives across a range of contexts: births, weddings, illnesses, and deaths. By employing such taken-for-granted ceremonies, rituals, or occasions as the framework within which I write about someone whose lived experience is not my own, I have found that I am better able to reflect on the biases and limitations that I bring to the creation.

For instance, had I used an ordinary event rather than action in *The Trials,* I might have tried to understand Candidate #2's life by writing about:

- A wedding or funeral for people he has come to know on the streets.
- A wedding or funeral for someone he was close with before he became homeless.

If these imaginations still felt too outside my understanding, I would have tried to craft everyday scenarios for Candidate #1—the character who is an embodiment of my own identity markers and positioning—and examined the ripple effects that might have been caused by Candidate #2's presence in those settings.

- What if she had to really, urgently use the bathroom with no other humans in sight except those sheltering in Candidate #2's encampment?
- What if Candidate #2 was sitting right by a table at which Candidate #1 is on a date?

The banal, the ordinary… they can be a gateway to understandings that, however limited, create space for nuance.

SCENE ELEVEN: INT. A ROOM

CANDIDATE #1 and CANDIDATE #2 are seated across from each other. They look into each other's eyes for one minute—a timer counts down from 60 seconds.

This time, both Candidates seem more comfortable looking into each other's eyes. What was visible awkwardness and discomfort in the first minute, what was an assumption of intentions and overflow of emotion, has now transformed into something more... playful.

CANDIDATE #1 is trying to figure out if there's enough of a dynamic between them for her to crack a smile. CANDIDATE #2 is also trying to ascertain the same thing. Did he see the ends of her mouth lifting ever so slightly?

Without knowing who is the one to extend the invitation and who is the one to receive it, both Candidates are smiling when the timer hits the 10-second mark.

WHEN THE TIMER HITS 0, CUT TO:

SCENE TWELVE: TO CAMERA

TEAM LEADER
You are going to participate in a Trial of your own now. I want you to look at the different faces around me.

A RANGE OF DIFFERENT FACES APPEAR LIKE A GALLERY ALL AROUND THE INSTRUCTOR. WHOSE ARE THE FACES? WELL, IT DEPENDS: ON THE CONTEXT IN WHICH THE SHOW IS BEING BROADCAST; ON THE PARTICULAR SOCIO-POLITICAL EVENTS THAT ARE HAPPENING IN THE WORLD AT THE TIME; ON THE VISION OF THE TEAM THAT IS CREATING A PRODUCTION OF THIS SCRIPT. THE FACES CAN EXPLICITLY SPEAK TO A SPECIFIC PLACE OR TIME. THEY CAN BE FICTIONAL OR ABSTRACT. FOR EXAMPLE:

- ALL THE FACES CAN BE OF THE SAME PERSON.
- THE FACES CAN BE OF THE ACTORS PLAYING THE TEAM MEMBERS.
- THEY CAN BE OF PEOPLE IN THE NEWS AT A GIVEN MOMENT. AT THE TIME OF WRITING THIS SCRIPT (26 FEBRUARY 2022), I IMAGINE THE GALLERY AS BEING COMPOSED OF FACES THAT FEATURE UKRAINIAN FAMILIES WHO ARE PROTESTING THE RUSSIAN INVASION OF THEIR COUNTRY.

TEAM LEADER (CONT'D)

Once I am done explaining the rules, I will invite you to use your remote control or your finger or whatever tool you're using to navigate this screen and pick a face from the ones you see around mine. Once you choose a face, you will get the opportunity to look into that person's eyes for sixty seconds.

If, before the timer runs out, you change your mind about looking at this person, you will have two options. You can either go back and choose someone else, or you can take the "I'm done for now" option and move on from this exercise.

Of course, there is a third option: once your sixty seconds with the first person ends, you might choose a second person from the gallery and repeat the one-minute exercise with them. Or maybe you'll want to choose the first person a second time, for an additional minute.

There is no wrong decision here. Just choices that say something about who we are in each moment. So, whatever choice you make, you might want to think about why you're making that particular decision.

Ready to begin?

Okay, which of these people's eyes would you like to gaze into for a minute? Use your remote control or your finger or whatever tool you're using to navigate this screen and pick a face from the ones you see around mine.

THE VIEWER HAS TO PICK A FACE TO BE ABLE TO CONTINUE WITH THE FILM. WHEN A FACE IS PICKED, A ZOOMED-IN IMAGE OF THE CHOSEN PERSON FILLS THE SCREEN.

A TIMER COUNTS DOWN, ON THE SCREEN, FROM 60 TO 0.

TWO OPTIONS ARE DISPLAYED BELOW THE FACE:

- "LOOK AGAIN" →IF THE VIEWER CHOOSES THIS OPTION THEY WILL BE TAKEN BACK TO THE MOSAIC OF FACES WHERE THEY CAN CHOOSE THE SAME/ DIFFERENT IMAGE.
- "I'M DONE FOR NOW" →IF THE VIEWER CHOOSES THIS OPTION, THEY WILL BE TAKEN TO THE NEXT SCENE OF THE TRIALS.

WHENEVER THE VIEWER CHOOSES
"I'M DONE FOR NOW," CUT TO:

Examine Scenes Eleven and Twelve: Choices

Examine the integration of choices for the audience and director/creator in *The Trials* especially within the scenes where the Team Leader speaks to the camera, and the viewer. What effect is fostered by the inclusion of a gallery of voices that the viewer can engage with in a way that is (at least at the time of this book's publication) *less* expected in the experience of viewing a film? To what extent is an integration of parallel narratives—the invitations extended to the viewer to engage in the action of looking at an Other; the options provided to the director/creator to weave in contexts and voices of their choosing—a strategic tool when an outsider-writer is responding to conditions they have no lived experience of?

How might invoking self-directed modes of engagement function as an additional pathway for a writer to be transparent about their lack of first-hand experience regarding the experience in question? Would *The Trials* be experienced differently without any of the scenes that are "To Camera" (scenes three, twelve, fourteen, and seventeen): why/how/why not?

What are ways to interpret the inclusion of options within the interactive components, where a director/creator of the screenplay can choose the composition of the visual galleries? What would have changed if—instead of offering choices where the faces in the gallery could represent images from a very specific place or time, be fictional or abstract or of the same person, or of people in the news at a given moment—the directions read: THERE ARE 24 FACES IN THE GALLERY, EACH OF SOMEONE WHO WAS IN UKRAINE ON 24 FEBRUARY 2022?

How might a decision to offer audience members and future directors/creators a range of different ways to engage with the text function to emphasize a *lack* of authorial expertise? To what extent might the multiple points of exploration that are offered *within* the test—for viewers, for potential creators—function as an outsider writer's acquiescence of authorial dominance?

However much authorial power is relinquished in a quest to ethically raise questions that are outside a writer's lived experience, how can sufficient structure and cohesion exist so that the work's central themes and questions are not lost in chaos?

SCENE THIRTEEN: THE CLASSROOM

The TEAM MEMBERS and their TEAM LEADER are seated around the same table.

VISUAL: THE TEAM IS WATCHING A RECORDING OF THE CANDIDATES LOOKING AT EACH OTHER. THE MORE OTHERWORLDLY THE VIDEO CAN BE, THE BETTER.

(When the recording reaches a specific moment, TEAM MEMBER #5 pauses the video.)

TEAM MEMBER #5
There. See? There. That's where it begins. With her.
Her mouth… the right side… see that twitch? That's where
it begins, I think. That's when she makes the offer of a smile, and he
takes her up on it.

TEAM MEMBER #8
Really? I don't know. Can you go back two seconds?
Yeah. There.
(TEAM MEMBER #5 rewinds the video and pauses it when
requested.)

See? He's the one who shows the hint of a smile first. And she
responds to that by… with her twitch or whatever.

TEAM MEMBER #6
Why do you two think it matters?

TEAM MEMBER #8
What?

TEAM MEMBER #6
Who started the smile? Why does it matter who started it?

TEAM MEMBER #5
Because… I don't know… because… it just seems like
something to note!

TEAM MEMBER #8
Well, because, maybe seeing who starts the move can tell us about which partner is more likely to want to continue the relationship after the gazing ends…?

TEAM LEADER
How so?

TEAM MEMBER #8
Well… if she's the one who started the smile and created… that you know… the first visible emotive moment after the awkwardness of that first minute… and if we see that she's the one who tries to reach out to him after they leave the Trial… if we note the same type of pattern in each pair, that the person who makes the first visible invitation to connect is the one who also initiates contact after the Trial… maybe we can predict which of the two Candidates in every iteration is more likely… to… you know… show long-term impact. And if we can tell that—

TEAM MEMBER #6
—right. Maybe we can then further narrow down the parameters of the kind of person we want to invite into the Trials itself.
(pause)

TEAM LEADER
Why might we want to be able to predict which kind of partici- pant to invite into the Trials?
(pause)

TEAM MEMBER #4
Just brainstorming here… but ummm… maybe having clearer parameters for the Candidate selection can… you know… can help us target the Trials more carefully… help us identify the kind of Candidates that are likely to achieve the kind of long-term impacts of empathy and connection that we're hoping that… you know… that the Trials will catalyse.

TEAM MEMBER #3
Or maybe even the opposite of that… right? Finding out this kind of pattern… maybe it's the people who are not already predisposed

to long-term impact that are the ones… that… you know… they're the ones who need to be the focus of the Trials. Not the ones who already have that tendency.

TEAM MEMBER #9

Or… I don't know… maybe there's something that we're not even seeing… maybe the patterns… seeing a trend in who makes the first move of visible reaching out… maybe there's some other tendency contained within that pattern that we don't even know to look for. A trend that could tell us more about… you know… I don't know. I don't even know if that makes sense.

TEAM MEMBER #10

No, that makes complete sense… and I really, I like that idea. We're looking not because we're hoping to find something specific; we're looking because we hope there is something to be found…

CUT TO:

SCENE FOURTEEN: TO CAMERA

TEAM LEADER

Do you find yourself wanting to know more about the person whose eyes you looked into earlier?

VIEWER IS PRESENTED WITH TWO OPTIONS ON THE SCREEN: "YES" AND "NO"

IF THE VIEWER CHOOSES "NO"

TEAM LEADER (CONT'D)

It's okay if your answer is no. But if you truly aren't the slightest bit curious about the person whose eyes you spent a minute looking into… ask yourself this: What would need to happen to make you curious? What would need to happen for you to wonder about a person who is different from you? What would need to happen to make you ask what brings them—this other person—to this place, to this time? What would need to happen to make you wonder about everything that lies behind the particular gaze their eyes held when

you looked into them? What would need to happen to make you
curious about someone who is not you?

AFTER THE TEAM LEADER'S SCRIPTED TEXT, CUT
TO: THE FOLLOWING SCENE IN THE CLASSROOM.
IF THE VIEWER CHOOSES "YES" THE GALLERY OF
FACES APPEARS AGAIN.

TEAM LEADER'S VOICE
Pick the person whose eyes you looked into earlier.

THE VIEWER NEEDS TO CHOOSE A FACE TO PROCEED.
WHEN THE FACE IS CHOSEN, THE PERSON'S IMAGE TAKES
OVER THE SCREEN AS THEY SHARE INFORMATION ABOUT
THEMSELVES:

WHO THEY ARE.

WHERE THEY ARE.

HOW THEY CAME TO BE THAT WAY.

THE THINGS THEY WANT THEIR GAZING PARTNER—IN THE
NON-TV WORLD—TO KNOW ABOUT THEM.

WHEN THE PERSON STOPS SPEAKING, CUT TO:

SCENE FIFTEEN: INT. A CLASSROOM

The TEAM MEMBERS are back in their classroom.
(silence)

TEAM LEADER
These are not bad outcomes.

TEAM MEMBER #2
They're not good outcomes either, are they?

TEAM MEMBER #10
They're not outcomes at all. Both Candidates essentially said, "I don't know."
That's literally like... no outcome!

TEAM LEADER
Look, these are called Trials for a reason. We are trying to figure something out. It's only to be expected that the first iteration of this new method is going to have... limitations.
(pause)

Let's consider this... in an ideal situation, if the Trials were to work, what would you want to see happening between these two Candidates? What kind of outcome would make you say: "Yes, this idea worked."
(pause)

TEAM MEMBER #8
For me, it would have been... if the educator, Candidate #1... if she was to have found a way to ensure that her Trial partner could get a job in her school. Like what Candidate #2 mentioned in his post-Trial debrief with you both.
(Gestures toward TEAM MEMBERS #3 and #4.)

TEAM MEMBER #6
I think that's asking for too much, though. We don't know the details about how he ended up on the street—there could be some reason why he couldn't find or keep a job until now... especially with his educational background. I mean... if she goes out on a limb like that for him and gets him a job and then... I don't know... something surfaces, something happens... I don't think that's the ideal, you know?
(pause)

TEAM MEMBER #5
To me, the ideal would be a desire for more connection. Like... if she was to show up at the street event next week... with a plan to... like... invite him to dinner once a week. Not even to her home—because she's already mentioned some concerns about that—but if

she makes a plan to meet with him somewhere public... that would be a way to address the second point he made... which was a great question, I thought... building for the foundation for a relationship that is not defined by the "home" of either one of the individuals.

TEAM MEMBER #1

What if... do you think it would work if he made a plan? Like, if she goes to visit him next week, he offers ways for them to stay connected and that way, he can define the kind of parameters that he'd be more comfortable with...

TEAM MEMBER #3

I see what you're saying but... in this situation... since she's the Candidate With More Privilege, I feel like it's on her to make the first move and to show him that she wants to connect more.

TEAM MEMBER #9

He's completely off the hook, then? The Candidate With Less Privilege has... there are no requirements for him to be... look, I'm not trying to be confrontational, but he's also an intelligent person. Why can't he be the one to put forward ideas for future engagement? Like... I don't know... don't get me wrong, I understand where you're coming from too, but... putting it on her to go there, with an idea that... that might be asking for too much... she's also not... she's not from here, she's also not like... the embodiment of all the privileges in the world... she has her scars and her wounds and her baggage... how can it only be on her?

TEAM MEMBER #7

How can you expect him to make any kind of "move" though? The man doesn't have a home to call his own—what can he possibly do to... to... make the first move in a way where his actions won't put him in danger of judgment... or... or... rejection... or even violence.
(silence)

TEAM MEMBER #2

Maybe we chose the wrong people.

TEAM LEADER
What do you mean?

TEAM MEMBER #2
We picked people who… maybe their worlds are too far apart
for anything but "I don't know" to be the outcome… you know?
I've been thinking about this a lot since our post-Trial conversation
with our Candidate… I know that it was intentional… that we were
asked to separately invite our respective Candidates, but maybe what
we needed to do was… maybe the four of us should have decided,
together, who we wanted to invite and… you know… like… I don't
know if I'm making sense.

TEAM MEMBER #7
You are… what you're saying, I think, is that if we—the four of
you, but maybe all of us, actually, as a team—if we had discussed
the Candidate selection together, we could have considered whether
these two people, even under the most successful of circumstances,
have the potential to continue a relationship outside the context of
the Trials. Does that sound something like what you were—

TEAM MEMBER #2
Yes! That's exactly it. Look, if we consider the differences
between people on a scale of one to ten right, where one is… people
who share incredibly similar visible and not-so-visible identity
markers—like siblings—and ten is people who are poles apart…
people who share no visible or invisible markers… I feel like our
Candidates are probably a ten.

TEAM MEMBER #3
So maybe that's the problem, then. Maybe we need to be picking
Candidate pairs that score somewhere in the middle of that difference scale. Two people who might be at a five, for example… where
they're different enough for the creation of empathy and long-term
connections to be necessary and meaningful… but also where
they're not so similar that they're likely to cross paths without any
intervention.

TEAM LEADER
That's a very interesting hypothesis…

TEAM MEMBER #10
I really like that idea.

TEAM MEMBER #5
Me too… I like that it doesn't sort of… essentialize difference.
Like… taking two people regardless of how great their differences
are… and saying that staring into each other's eyes for four
minutes will create some kind of lasting… anything. I like that
it—what did you just call it, a differences scale; love it—I really
like that this approach would force us to question… you know…
what kinds of empathy can lead to more long-term outcomes than
others?
(All TEAM MEMBERS show their agreement with this idea in
verbal and non-verbal ways.)

TEAM LEADER
Okay, so we seem to be having some kind of consensus here. We
need to be more intentional in how we pick Candidates… there
should be some balance of how similar and dissimilar they are from
each other. A five on a scale of one to ten. That's a great idea for us
to pass up to the Analysis team for some more feedback. But before
we do, we need to consider something: how do we assess differences
on a scale? How would we frame that "calculation," if I can call
it that?
(silence)

TEAM MEMBER #6
What if… what if we considered the ideal outcomes, right? So,
when we're discussing a pairing—and I think whoever said this was
right, we might need to discuss the pairings as a team rather than just
pairs for this to work… so when we're discussing a pairing, what if
we intentionally ask ourselves how the two Candidates could take
their relationship forward if they wanted to—we use this hypothet-
ical as a way to assess how different they are on a one to ten scale—
assuming we stay with that scale, just for now.

TEAM MEMBER #2
A hypoth—like we just did for this Candidate pair, just now,
you mean?

TEAM MEMBER #6
Exactly. We ask what an ideal post-Trial outcome would look
like for two potential Candidates. Because just now, as soon as we
tried to figure that out for Candidates #1 and #2, we immediately
realized the struggles, right? We immediately realized that even if
both of them have the seed of interest, there are too many contextual
conditions that are likely to prohibit a longer-term relationship from
actually becoming a reality.

TEAM LEADER
I see... so let's explore that idea a little more. Let's say the
premise remains the same, for someone with more privilege and
someone with less privilege to make a connection with each other.
And just for the sake of this thought exercise, let's say we stay
with Candidate #1 as one member of our duo. If we wanted to
identify a second Candidate who would not be as far from her on
a difference scale—as Candidate #2 turned out to be—how might
we have gone about it? What characteristics would such a person
have embodied?
(pause)

TEAM MEMBER #3
I wonder if... what if we had chosen someone who shared a
similar like... living situation as Candidate #2... but it was someone
who shared her heritage? Like... someone from her country or her
part of the world who has... you know... for whatever reason and
circumstances, come to live on the streets here.

VISUAL: AS TEAM MEMBERS HYPOTHESIZE ABOUT
DIFFERENT CANDIDATE TYPES BELOW, THEIR CONSIDE-
RATIONS ARE ACCOMPANIED BY SHIFTING IMAGES THAT
SHOWCASE THE DESCRIPTORS THEY CONSIDER.

TEAM MEMBER #9
Right… maybe the shared ancestry would have created more possible overlaps rather than differences… I could see that.

TEAM MEMBER #1
Yeah… maybe that would have enabled both of them to be more… to have more faith that the other person could be someone they could learn from, or with, in the long run… I say that but then I also wonder if shared ancestry… like, the Candidate herself described how she had a different set of ideas about people who lived on the streets where she grew up… so ancestry could actually have… like… led to preconceived notions that are harder to break through because they're cemented by… like… like… cultural baggage… ?
(pause)

TEAM MEMBER #2
Maybe gender then? Rather than ancestry? Or both? If she connected with someone who shared the same heritage and gender as herself, someone who also happened to live on the street, maybe there would… there would be more ways to see themselves in each other… maybe gender is another aspect here that adds to how Candidate #1 sees concerns about inviting our existing Candidate #2 into her home… or spending time with him alone… I only know the stereotypes, but I think there's quite a separation of genders where she's from, no?
(pause)

TEAM MEMBER #6
Apart from those sorts of visible identity markers, I would say we might have considered the context in which she wor—

TEAM MEMBER #9
Yes! Sorry, I didn't mean to interrupt you—

TEAM MEMBER #6
It's okay, please—go on.

TEAM MEMBER #9
So, if we went with that shared context idea, we might have considered who the people with less privilege in the school context

are, that Candidate #1 might be less likely to interact with... so if she's a teacher, maybe the Candidate most suitable to be paired with her is someone who works on the custodial or janitorial staff at a school. Maybe her school. Maybe some other school. But that way, the shared work context becomes a way for the one to see the other as a means of... solidarity in some way... making it less impossible to visualize the possibility of a relationship that goes beyond the time they spend together in the Trials.

TEAM MEMBER #6

Yup. And we could be even more careful there. Not only is it someone in a role at the school that she's less likely to interact with... maybe it's someone who is also an immigrant, and who is also the same gender. That way, there are many things in common that balance with the other characteristics that... you know... create rifts between them in the real world...

(pause)

TEAM LEADER

Okay. These are all excellent starting points for what shifts we might want to make to the next Trial. What's the first step? Where do we start?

CUT TO:

SCENE SIXTEEN: INT. AND EXT. SPLIT SCREEN

CANDIDATE #1 and CANDIDATE #2, each on different sides of the screen, in their own worlds.

CANDIDATE #1 is cooking, pottering around in her home, looking out of the window. She watches shadowy figures outside, of people living on the streets below.

CANDIDATE #2 is setting up a temporary shelter for the night. His attention is captured when someone who looks like CANDIDATE #1 walks past his resting place for the night. It's not her; he turns his attention back to his current task.

CUT TO:

SCENE SEVENTEEN: TO CAMERA

TEAM LEADER

I want you to turn to the person sitting next to you and answer
three questions. If there's no one sitting next to you, talk to me. Out
loud. It doesn't matter that I can't hear you. All that matters is that
you can hear yourself.

Ready?

What do you think people see when they look at you?

ON-SCREEN INSTRUCTION: HIT PAUSE TILL YOU ARE
READY FOR THE NEXT QUESTION

What do you wish people *would* see when they look at you?

ON-SCREEN INSTRUCTION: HIT PAUSE TILL YOU ARE
READY FOR THE NEXT QUESTION

What needs to change—in the world, in yourself—for you to get
from how you think you are seen to how you wish to be?

FADE TO BLACK.

**Examine Scenes Thirteen to Seventeen: Unresolved
Endings**

Examine how I have chosen to conclude *The Trials:* for the
Candidates, for the team conducting the Trials, and for the
viewer who is invited to engage with the gallery of images and
voices.

There are no clean resolutions here, for anyone. No cul-
mination of the Candidates' engagement suggests anything
more than new questions for both of them; nothing more than
a carrying on of their lives as they were before, perhaps with

just a little more nuance in each character's understanding of the other.

What if *The Trials* had ended with Candidates #1 and #2 becoming friends and sustaining a visible relationship beyond their time gazing at each other? What if *The Trials* had ended with the Team Members coming to certain conclusions about the efficacy of their efforts, with concrete answers for their research questions? What are the risks of endings with firm(er) resolutions, especially for authors who write about contexts that they have not lived?

To what extent might unresolved endings represent a more ethical way for outsiders to write about lives that lie outside the realms of their own experience?

Section Two

Explore Global Voices

As you go through this section, use the QR code or the footnoted link to visit the online forum for this book and share thoughts or questions from your explorations.[1]

1 https://nanditadinesh.com/creative-writing-and-the-experiences-of-others

DOI: 10.4324/9781032688749-3

Part One

Explore Allegories and Abstractions

Rewrite the three texts that follow in a way that makes their content general, and applicable to a range of contexts, rather than being specific to the countries or regions they currently address. As you craft your responses, consider these questions:

What kind of license does the creation of allegory permit the writer who does not have the lived experience of the context in question? What liberties can a writer take without falling victim to appropriation, over-simplification, or sensationalism?

Conversely, how might a non-specific approach dilute the poignancy that comes from an emphasis on the specific? How might approaches of allegorizing and abstraction risk a problematic otherworldliness of struggles that are all too real?

Are there specific kinds of events or incidences—or particular degrees of "insider-ness" and "outsider-ness" with regard to the author's lived experience—that make the use of allegories and abstractions more or less ethically murky? If you're not sure where to start, remember there are starting points provided at the end of each article.

Text One

Myanmar Junta Grants Partial Pardon to Detained Leaders Amid Continuing Crisis and Resistance

> *This story by Mong Palatino (2023) originally appeared on Global Voices.*

DOI: 10.4324/9781032688749-4

Myanmar's military authorities released more than 7,000 prisoners and granted a partial pardon to deposed leaders Aung San Suu Kyi and Win Myint during a Buddhist religious celebration. Critics say this move was intended to ease international pressure and weaken the opposition.

The military grabbed power in February 2021 and immediately detained State Counsellor Aung San Suu Kyi and President Win Myint. It vowed to restore civilian rule by holding an election, but more than two years later, the country remains under an extended state of emergency while the junta has violently suppressed all forms of dissent. Despite the crackdown targeting the opposition, the military has failed to stabilize its rule as pro-democracy forces have continued to garner public support. Anti-junta activists and ethnic armed groups have launched campaigns undermining the military dictatorship. Meanwhile, independent media outlets have consistently exposed the brutality of the junta and the impact of the conflict across the country. Myanmar's military authorities are also unable to get diplomatic recognition and the support of the majority of the international community.

Amid the intensifying crisis, the military government released 7,749 prisoners in time for Dhammasetkya Day, which commemorates the first sermon ever delivered by the Buddha. But the Assistance Association of Political Prisoners reported that only 120 political prisoners were included in the amnesty, while according to its tally, 19,733 individuals arrested since the coup remain imprisoned. The partial pardon granted to Aung San Suu Kyi and Win Myint will not lead to their release, since the former has been convicted in 14 other cases, while the latter's prison term was only reduced by four years. The opposition spokesperson described the pardon as "cosmetic." He added that "the move comes straight out of the regime's dirty politics playbook to ease international pressure." In an editorial, the news website *Myanmar Now* noted that the junta is using an old tactic to distract opposition forces and confuse the international community. "All of this is straight out of the playbook of previous regimes," the news outlet stated. "Use Suu Kyi to create the illusion that the military might be willing to soften its position, and then deploy this fiction to weaken domestic resistance and divide international opinion."

Australian economist Sean Turnell, who was previously detained after the coup for being an adviser of the former government, also mocked the pardon issued by the junta. He insisted that the deposed leaders should not have been arrested in the first place. "Myanmar's problems will not be solved by reducing the prison sentences on people who should never have been sentenced in the first place," Turnell said. "Real change is possible in Myanmar, but it will not come from applauding meaningless gestures, as attractive as they might be as click-bait. As with such online temptations broadly, best not to hit the like button until there is truly something to be happy about."

In an editorial, the news website *The Irrawaddy* described the pardon as "appalling but laughable" and urged the international community to step up its pressure against the junta. Indeed, if ASEAN (Association of Southeast Asian Nations) and the international community want to see a restoration of stability and peace in Myanmar, it is time to increase, not reduce, the pressure on the regime and support the democratic opposition. All players should demand the immediate release of Suu Kyi and other detained leaders of the ousted government, as well as elected MPs and all other political prisoners.

Not Sure Where to Start?

Rewrite the text with the sole difference of replacing all identifiers in the text with generic terms of what those names or terms symbolize. For example:

- Replace "Myanmar" with "The State"
- "Junta" and "military" with "The Guardsmen"
- "Aung San Suu Kyi" and "Win Myint" with their titles of "State Counsellor" and "President"
- "Media" with "The Observers" or "The Witnesses"

Can a simple shift of nomenclature alter how you navigate your personal, authorial compass when writing about Myanmar?

Text Two

Life during the Pandemic: An Interview with Former Refugee, Exiled Cartoonist Eaten Fish

> *This story by Mong Palatino (2021) originally appeared on Global Voices.*

Iranian cartoonist Ali Dorani, whose pen name is Eaten Fish, was one of nine cartoonists awarded a work grant by the Norway-based Fritt Ord Foundation in recognition of his work in using satire as a visual expression and medium of criticism in society. Ali Dorani sought asylum in Australia in 2013 but he was transferred to Manus Island, an offshore detention camp in Papua New Guinea, where he was forced to stay as a refugee for four years before he was allowed to relocate to Norway in December 2017 through the sponsorship of the International Cities of Refuge Network.

Dorani's cartoon depicting the struggle of refugees in Manus was widely published. Highlighting stories of persecution inside Australia's borders, Dorani's creation brought attention to policies that are usually missed in more dominant narratives of Australia being one of the freest countries in the world. Recognizing the power of Dorani's creation, in 2016, the Cartoonists Rights Network International granted him the Courage in Editorial Cartooning Award for his work.

In 2018, Global Voices interviewed Ali Dorani about his difficult transition from being a refugee in Manus to his new life in Norway. We caught back up with him to learn about his latest artwork that landed him the grant, his experience during the coronavirus pandemic, and his work of the past three years.

"I have had many galleries in different cities in Norway and also in other countries such as Germany and Sweden," Dorani told us. "I've had a huge audience by now. I think over 15,000 people and students have visited my galleries, talks and conversations."

Dorani has also written about how the pandemic has disrupted his life as an exiled artist and former refugee who relies on public events to share his story and artworks.

"As a freelance artist the pandemic damaged my work so much because I have to show my drawings to the public and I have to talk to the public and I have to share cartoons with them, but the pandemic restricted me so much." He goes on to explain how after the pandemic, "I was not able to travel much, and I was not able to run galleries." Dorani was forced to "look for a permanent job, [but] because of the pandemic, finding a new job was almost impossible for me."

Recently, Dorani was informed about a competition organized by The Fritt Ord foundation regarding the theme of majority and minority. He remembered having a hard time understanding the topic: "It is absolutely so difficult really talking about minorities and majorities because, for example, I don't really know in what context

I should translate these two words." Dorani further explains his difficulty understanding this binary by asking: "Do minorities or majorities exist, or do they mean the opposite of each other? Do we actually understand these two words? Or do we totally understand what exactly a minority or majority is? It was my first time coming up with such a thing." With only two days to work on his submission, Dorani explained how he came up with the symbol of a sunflower to represent the human race.

I came up with drawing a sunflower because a sunflower is a flower that has hundreds of seeds inside itself which represents the Society in my cartoon. I drew seven sunflowers in a cage which represent the different continents and I called them the minority... And on the other side I drew one sunflower which represents the majority. The black and white sunflower represents a small group who has the power to control the rest of the world and... So, you see the black and white sunflower has a key and the rest of the sunflowers in the cage are locked. So, because the black and white sunflower has the power, I call it the majority and the rest of the sunflowers that don't have the power are being called the minority.

Dorani's sunflower creation ultimately won him the award and inspired him to pursue his unfinished projects—his books—and publish them. "I have been writing a book about my life and the history I have from the refugee detention centres in Australia and immigration prison camps in Papua New Guinea and also, I'm doing another comic book about my life in Norway and now I'm so motivated to finish these two books."

When asked about one major piece of advice to fellow artists who are struggling to survive the pandemic, here is what Dorani has to say: "I would like to tell other fellow (artists) that they should never stop trying, they should never stop searching and they should never be afraid of sharing their opinion, especially cartoonists."

Not Sure Where to Start?

Choose one or two instances from the account of Dorani's journey to Norway and consider how you might write about it only using sound and movement. Which sounds or songs or melodies capture what strikes you most powerfully about Dorani's journey? How would you write these sounds or songs or melodies through words: as transcriptions of lyrics? As transliterations of melodies? As blank pages punctuated by symbols that aim to show motion or containment?

Who or what would move in response to the soundscape you've crafted? How might you use words to describe their movements? Which members of this textual ensemble will move fluidly and which of them will move in jerky discord? Who or what will start, and who or what will follow?

Once you have written your choreography, consider to what extent your sound- and movement-centred text has been able to address what you sought to capture about Dorani's journey, while also mitigating the risk of portraying an embodied understanding that you might not have.

Text Three

Undertones: If on Welfare, Better Learn Dutch and Be a Man

> *This story by Civic Media Observatory (2023)*
> *originally appeared on Global Voices.*

Data scientist Ingelse analysed the discussions about algorithms in the Netherlands. This is a big deal in that country: in 2021, the government fell after years of mishandling a case of AI fraud detection among childcare beneficiaries. Thousands of families, primarily of migrant backgrounds, had been wrongly accused of cheating the system. The Netherlands, a country that takes pride in efficiency and the use of technology in government services, is a case study of how the misuse of AI can hurt the lives of individuals and undermine trust in authorities.

Algorithms continue to be used in municipalities throughout the Netherlands to determine who is more or less likely to commit welfare fraud—an endless hot topic in Europe. However, nearly all of this technology is opaque to journalists and researchers as authorities claim privacy and intellectual property concerns. Only Rotterdam, the second-largest Dutch city, recently agreed to share the skeleton of their algorithm with journalists from investigative media Lighthouse

Reports and Follow the Money. They accidentally also shared the training data sets, which provided invaluable insight into how the algorithm works from the inside out. As a result, the journalists found that the algorithm is a scoring card fed with personal criteria such as age, sex, and marital status, as well as elements of behaviour and language skills. Rotterdam initially developed its algorithm with the help of consulting firm Accenture.

"The data fed into the algorithm ranges from invasive (the length of someone's last romantic relationship) and subjective (someone's ability to convince and influence others) to banal (how many times someone has emailed the city) and seemingly irrelevant (whether someone plays sports)," Lighthouse writes. In other words, if you are a) a woman, b) plurilingual, c) twenty- or thirty-something, and d) a parent, the algorithm would file you as someone at risk of committing fraud, independently of any actual fraudulent behaviour in the past. If you appear shy to the social worker, you will be even worse off. You will not know whether you're on the blacklist, or why. Still, uncomfortable investigations by local authorities would ensue, as well as potentially losing welfare benefits. "The Dutch tend to believe they don't have structural racism, whereas this algorithm clearly shows otherwise, as people with limited Dutch proficiency are discriminated against," Ingelse says. Other discriminatory algorithm uses in the Netherlands have also come to light, with the profiling of nationality and ethnicity in visa applications.

Algorithmic bias is not new. Journalists have pointed out the intrinsic biases in algorithmic risk scores elsewhere. As early as 2016, an investigation by ProPublica revealed that within the US criminal justice system, black individuals were twice as likely to be erroneously identified as "high risk" for reoffending; in contrast, white individuals were twice as likely to be wrongly categorized as "low risk." In the Rotterdam case, experts argue that AI performance is only marginally better than randomly selecting welfare beneficiaries for investigation, according to Lighthouse. AI algorithms exhibit bias due to training on skewed or insufficient real-world data and the influence of human developers' inherent prejudice. Biases enter the system in other ways too.

How Do People Perceive These Revelations?

In the Dutch AI scandals, the public debate does not tend to happen via original tweets or posts, but rather only in comment sections which, surprisingly, show an interesting array of opinions. Most of those launching the debate are journalists.

"It could be that the Dutch are tired after the Toeslagenaffaire [childcare benefits scandal], and are more focused on ChatGPT," Ingelse says. "Also, public figures who have been part of the scandals tactically avoid answering questions about their involvement." He adds that the only people burdened with these specific algorithms are minorities, who are often invisibilized. "Notice how these fraud algorithms are never used in profit taxes, for example, which would target the rich," Ingelse says. Local Rotterdam authorities were contacted for a response, as were newly created groups of families impacted by the algorithm to understand their perspectives; no responses were received.

Narrative 1: "Algorithms That Help Fight Crime Should Be Implemented Even if Biased"

This narrative in a nutshell: "The algorithm is doing its job." It implies that the algorithm works, even if flawed, in fighting fraud. This discourse has been around for years. For example, at the height of the childcare benefits scandal in 2019, far-right blogger Pim Beaart, alias "Hannibal," argued in an editorial piece that politicians only "want to use algorithms when they validate their political opinions." More recently, one of the largest conservative Dutch opinion magazines, *EW*, claimed that automated decisions in visa applications should be the norm, despite always targeting people from certain nationalities such as former Dutch colony Suriname. On Facebook, they ask: "Shouldn't the government just use digital programs that dare to filter [visa applicants] in cold blood?" Others, such as the famous media blog GeenStijl also argue in favour of efficiency, one of the most popular overarching narratives in the Netherlands.

"The Dutch consider themselves to favour efficiency above anything else," Ingelse says. The Netherlands is leading the way in implementing digital IDs, incorporating technology in education and healthcare, and advancing governmental digitalization. Whatever they do—and how they deal with algorithmic biases—might influence how other countries develop their own AI. However, few understand the basics of algorithms. "Besides the expected presence of xenophobic comments and racism, this narrative will probably always be present as long as people don't understand how algorithms work and the difference between objective data and the interpretation of that data," Ingelse says. Correlation does not mean causation.

Narrative 2: "Dutch Authorities Are Harming Their Citizens By Using Discriminatory Algorithms"

This narrative in a nutshell: "Stop using discriminatory AI." In tweets and in comments, people claim that the Netherlands has a history of discriminatory algorithms that re-victimize vulnerable populations. Focusing on someone's poor Dutch skills, is, for many, a subtext for targeting immigrants. Some go further by stating that "Algorithms should be open and transparent to ensure they are not biased." This is not the case for the vast majority of algorithms out there. So, while people criticized Rotterdam's algorithm use, many also lauded the city for at least sharing their algorithm with the journalists.

Most of these posts and comments come from people defending human rights, not the people directly impacted by the algorithms themselves. That is perhaps precisely because vulnerable populations are less visible online, or less vocal (in Dutch) online. However, when directly interviewed, people are very opinionated against the use of discriminatory AI. Dutch outlet Vers Breton went to Rotterdam's market, where people with less economic means go, and interviewed shoppers, who all criticized the use of algorithms. Dutch legislators are also pushing for more AI regulation. "The central problem with AI development is that it's entirely market-driven: it's a multibillion-dollar industry with no rules," Kim van Sparrentak, a member of the European Parliament with the Greens/EFA group writes in an extensive Twitter/X thread.

Not Sure Where to Start?

Write a stream-of-consciousness text as if spoken, thought, or imagined by an algorithm that is being used to determine an individual's likelihood to commit fraud. Invite your non-human, algorithm-spewing protagonist's ramblings to showcase its capacity for regurgitating the biases of the humans that created it.

You can situate your algorithm in the context of the welfare system in the Netherlands. You could just as well make it about systemic biases within the technological apparatuses that control the criminal justice system in the United States. Or about the algorithms being deployed to predict religious bias in India.

Can the non-human be a writer's more ethical foray into others' realities? When writing about existences that we have not experienced, might we be better positioned *not* to start with the lives of the humans we can never be, but instead, the non-human objects in those settings—a wall, a window, a cloud, an algorithm?

Through voicing the non-human, might we be able to reveal our limited vision of others' experiences while still not shying away from the very human enigmas before us?

Works Cited

Civic Media Observatory. (2023). *Undertones: If on welfare, better learn Dutch and be a man.* [Online] Global Voices. Available at: https://globalvoices.org/2023/06/29/undertones-if-on-welfare-better-learn-dutch-and-be-a-man/ [Accessed 28 Aug. 2023].

Palatino, M. (2021). *Life during the pandemic: An interview with former refugee, exiled cartoonist Eaten Fish.* [Online] Global Voices. Available at: https://globalvoices.org/2021/09/24/life-during-the-pandemic-an-interview-with-former-refugee-exiled-cartoonist-eaten-fish/ [Accessed 28 Aug. 2023].

Palatino, M. (2023). *Myanmar junta grants partial pardon to detained leaders amid continuing crisis and resistance.* [Online] Global Voices. Available at: https://globalvoices.org/2023/08/06/myanmar-junta-grants-partial-pardon-to-detained-leaders-amid-continuing-crisis-and-resistance/ [Accessed 28 Aug. 2023].

Part Two

Explore Autoethnography

Write autoethnographic response pieces to each of the three news stories that follow.

What is autoethnography? Very simply, autoethnography might be understood as a process—or a range of strategies—rooted in the excavation of an individual's perspectives, lived experiences, or biases in relation to the experiences of others.

Writers of autoethnography seek to make evident, in their writing, their own limited perspectives which inform their words. Written autoethnographies, through a transparent demonstration of humility and limitation, invite readers to see the text as nothing more or less than one flawed human's attempt to understand the life of another.

As you write autoethnographic responses to the texts in this section, consider these questions:

To what extent does the inclusion of autoethnography in writing about the lives of others function as a mode of ethical engagement in which unknown lives are not shied away from but rather, explicitly shared alongside the limited perspectives that shape their creation?

How can the inclusion of autoethnography evade or navigate the risk of self-indulgence: of making what is about the others, too much about the self?

Consider the use of an implicit form of autoethnography, as in the framework of *The Trials*, to the more explicit forms that are presented in the starting point ideas to the articles that follow. Are there particular degrees of "insider-ness" and

DOI: 10.4324/9781032688749-5

"outsider-ness" with regard to the author's lived experience that might make either implicit or explicit autoethnography more suitable?

Text Four

Can Algerian Human Rights Defenders Be Safe in Tunisia?

This story by Saoussen Ben Cheikh (2023)
originally appeared on Global Voices.

The time in the 1990s when Algeria was proudly renowned for having "the freest press in the Arab world" seems far away now. Crackdowns on freedom of expression and financial hardships in the last twenty years have forced many broadsheets, such as *Le Matin, La Tribune,* and the weekly *La Nation*, to shut down. The climate, in fact, no longer supports freedom. Despite toppling Abdelaziz Bouteflika's two-decade-long reign in 2019, the Algerian path to democracy was soon aborted by current president Abdelmadjid Tebboune. In June 2021, Tebboune made changes to the penal code in Algeria, further broadening the definition of "terrorism" in article 87. The expansion includes "to work for or to incite by any means, to accede to power or change the system of governance by non-constitutional means" and to "harm the integrity of national territory or to incite doing so, by any means."

Authorities have since used this article to prosecute an increasing number of activists, journalists, and human rights defenders. According to human rights organizations, over 280 activists and dozens of journalists are languishing in detention, mostly for charges of defamation of politicians or because of publications on social networks. Additionally, many others have gone into exile. The Algerian regime aims to demonstrate, by example, that it can strike hard. The latest instance was the conviction of journalist Ihsane El Kadi in June 2023. As a leader of one of the last independent press groups in Algeria—Interface Médias, which includes Radio M and the news website Maghreb Émergent—he was convicted on charges of "receiving funds for political propaganda" and "harming the national security of the state" then sentenced to seven years in prison following an appeal. Interface Médias was fined and shut down, and its assets were seized.

The criminalization of freedom of expression sends a frightening signal to anyone daring to report a different view from the official narrative. According to Boukhlef, an Algerian journalist at Liberté, as mentioned in The New Arab: "In recent years we have been forced into self-censorship. Journalists have been imprisoned for reporting. The pressures on media managers pushed us to be careful about what we write." Algeria is currently ranked at the bottom, 136th out of 180, in the Reporters Without Borders (RSF) 2023 World Press Freedom Index.

Repression of Dissenting Voices at Home and Abroad

Following a classic authoritarian playbook, Algerian authorities are not only cracking down on dissident voices at home but are also targeting them abroad, including in next door Tunisia. Algeria has the leverage to pressure Tunisia, finding a friendly echo with Tunisian president Kais Saied, who is also enforcing a clampdown on dissidents. There are dangerous precedents of opponents fleeing repression and seeking safety in Tunisia, only to be hunted down by the Algerian authorities. One such case involves Algerian activist and Christian convert Slimane Bouhafs, who spent almost two years in an Algerian prison before being released in March 2018.

Following his release, Bouhafs entered Tunisia legally where he was granted political refugee status by the United Nations High Commissioner for Refugees (UNHCR) in 2020, theoretically providing him protection, as international law prohibits returning anyone to a country where they may face persecution or human rights violations. In August 2021, unidentified men abducted Bouhafs from his home in Tunis and forcibly returned him to Algeria, where he was sentenced to three years' imprisonment. Despite calls from human rights organizations, no investigation has been launched into this grave violation of the principle of non-refoulement and international refugee law. Tunisia has not commented on the issue.

Similarly, human rights defender Zakaria Hannache, known for documenting state repression under the Hirak has found refuge in Tunisia since November 2022. He is escaping false charges of "praising terrorism" and "undermining national unity," for which he faces up to

35 years in prison. He was also granted political refugee status by the UNHCR. But Zakaria still feels unsafe; he is in fact hiding in Tunisia and has changed his address at least 13 times. In an interview with *Le Monde*, he expressed his fear of "being kidnapped by the Algerian authorities." He is now petitioning France for protection.

Tunisian Dependence on Its "Big Sister" Algeria

Tunisia's relationship with Algeria, its "big sister," has never been better. It is to Algeria that President Kais Saied made his first state visit shortly after he was elected in 2019. Tebboune was the first Arab president to call Saied after his power grab on 25 July 2021, which involved suspending the parliament, dissolving the government, and taking control of the judiciary. Since then, the country has been grappling with just about everything from a sinking economy and rampant corruption to social tensions. It is on the verge of bankruptcy and struggling to provide basic commodities. President Saied has resisted concessions to secure a rescue package. He has been hostile to international lenders and the IMF, which demands reforms and political liberalization. Refusing the "diktats that come from abroad and cause only more impoverishment," he suggested, "the alternative is that we must rely on ourselves." He turned to Algeria for backup.

Additionally, Tunisia relies on Algeria for its national security and most of its electricity. Algeria's list of services to its neighbours is indeed long and is always ready to jump in and rescue. According to political analyst, Jamil Sayah, in an article on TV5 Monde, "Algerian power has made itself indispensable to Tunisian power. It assures [Tunisian] survival." Sayah contextualizes this power dynamic by sharing that the "increase in gas and oil prices gave more financial margins to Algiers, and, in the end, the nearly 700 million dollars in the form of loans or donations is little for Algiers." Money that, Sayah says, allows for Kais Saied "to stay afloat."

The Complicity of Tunisia

This heavy dependence on its Algerian neighbour puts Tunisia in a fragile position. Algiers expects Tunis to fulfil its demands in return for support. However, it is not always straightforward. In February 2023, when prominent Hirak activist Amira Bouraoui entered Tunisia illegally to escape a two-year sentence for "offending Islam and insulting the president," Tunisia allowed her to flee to France, despite Algerian pressures for her extradition. The decision angered the Algerian government and sparked a diplomatic row. In retaliation, Algerian customs immediately held 200 Tunisian cars and confiscated goods at the border. The next day, Tunisian Foreign Minister Othman Jerandi was dismissed without explanation, leading many to suspect that he was sacrificed to appease Algerian anger. For now, thanks to their significant oil supply, the Algerian authorities can maintain the political status quo at home and in neighbouring Tunisia. However, the Amira Bouraoui episode demonstrated that there is still room to push back. Despite its democratic backsliding, Tunisia can still rely on its strong civil society and independent media to report violations and pressure for the protection of human rights defenders at home and for anyone seeking safety.

Not Sure Where to Start?

Write a letter to Ihsane El Kadi.

Start with whatever aspect of your identity might resonate with something you perceive as being related to his. Write to Kadi about what might enable you to understand at least some small part of this experience. Perhaps you have a shared profession. Or a shared experience of censorship. Or a shared gender. Or shared nationality. Or a shared something else. How does this one aspect, one facet, one experience, one instance enable you to approach a sliver of understanding about El Kadi?

And then, in the same breath—with the same weight—write about what makes your understanding limited: what layers are you *not* able to imagine, within the very marker that you might share with him. For instance: if you share Kadi's profession, what about your experience of journalism limits you from understanding his? If censorship is the shared thread, what seems different in each of your experiences of it? If nationality enables you to approach an understanding of him, what might make you both different kinds of Algerians?

In your letter, alongside your solidarity with that which is familiar, tell Kadi about that which remains alien: the aspects of his life and encounters that you might never be able to imagine.

If there is absolutely nothing about Kadi and his experience that you think you can come close to understanding, write a letter about exactly that. Tell him about the many divides that separate you from being able to even imagine a resonance with him. Articulate to him how the things that make you who you are, create a barrier from being able to access anything that seems true to who he is. What is it about who you are makes who he is (who you understand him to be, of course) completely inaccessible? And what might stand to be gained by gazing into that abyss?

Text Five

Disinformation Helps Weaponize Homophobia in the Balkans

This story by Global Voices Central & Eastern Europe
(2023) originally appeared on Global Voices.

Populist political forces across Europe have been utilizing homophobia and the stigmatization of LGBTQ+ people as a weapon of political influence for the last two decades. Many of these campaigns have mimicked, or were even helped by, extreme right-wing circles from the US.

After 2013, Moscow emerged as a major generator of homophobic narratives that exploited existing endemic intolerance in the Balkans region. A recent analysis entitled "Kremlin speaking: homophobia as geopolitics" by Bulgarian fact-checking platform Factcheck.bg, run by the Association of European Journalists-Bulgaria (AEJ), revealed that key homophobic narratives pushed by Kremlin propaganda are meant to undermine trust in the European Union (EU) by stoking fears among socially conservative people. "The West imposes homosexuality and paedophilia on us," one narrative stated. "Membership in the European Union (EU) means acceptance of same-sex marriage;" or "European values contradict traditional morality." The author, Bulgarian editor and journalist, Vanessa Nikolova, points out that Moscow is using homophobia as a geopolitical weapon, as an extension of its state policy of protection of "traditional values." In December 2022, the Russian Federation adopted amendments to the federal information law banning "LGBTQ+ propaganda" and blocking web resources.

Nikolova points out that today's Russian social media users often use the expression "gay-Nazism" when discussing the political situation in Ukraine and in Western countries. She also noted the development of a whole new propaganda vocabulary, fitting the definition of "newspeak" from George Orwell's novel *Nineteen Eighty-four*.

Words like "Gayrope," "Eurogay," "liberast," "tolerast" (the last two referring to the Bulgarian word for "faggot" combined with liberal and tolerance), etc. are recognizable in the anti-democratic and anti-European rhetoric in Bulgaria. This propaganda vocabulary began to penetrate the Bulgarian media as early as 2013 but reached the peak of its popularity in 2018 in the debates on the adoption of the Istanbul Convention. Then the word "gender" was created and imposed—a negative name for people with nontraditional sexual orientation, as well as for those who sympathize with them, and in a broader sense—for human rights defenders, civil society, and supporters of liberal values in general.

Nikolova warned that the basis for these narratives is the suggestion that the EU is morally unacceptable and destroys traditional values. "By exporting 'homophobic nationalism,' Russia is carrying out a much more comprehensive plan—to undermine the foundations of European liberal democracies based on the principles of respect for human rights and tolerance." She further explains that due to this "European values are presented as focused solely on the rights of sexual minorities, and the EU is accused of carrying out 'gender propaganda.'" Nikolova pointed out that in the Balkans, disinformation narratives against "Gayrope," degradation, and "Satanism," have gained traction in socially conservative and nationalistic circles. The ripple effect of the official Russian rhetoric, which presents the war in Ukraine as an extension of this policy by other means, has an impact among Kremlin proxies in the Balkans, promoting the myths of "innocent" Russia and the "wrong" West, and generating outrage based on fear and prejudice.

Articles by the Western Balkans Anti-Disinformation Hub project document that such narratives affect not only communities of Slavic peoples (Serbs, Macedonians, Montenegrins, and Bulgarians), considered culturally linked to Russia via Orthodox Christianity, but also communities that might be historically considered adverse to Russian imperialism, such as ethnic Albanians in Kosovo, North Macedonia, and Albania, as well as ethnic Bosniaks in Bosnia and Herzegovina. When such propaganda targets socially conservative groups, like majority-Muslim communities, the primary goal is not to make them love Vladimir Putin more, or to generate open support for the Russian regime. The aim is to exploit homophobia to incite fear and outrage against the West and democracy, creating further discord and disrupting the Euro-Atlantic integration of the region. For instance, disinformation presenting the EU as weak and disunited includes lies about measures against LGBTQ+ people supposedly adopted by the Italian parliament, spread in Kosovo in March 2022 and in North Macedonia in June 2023.

During the last two years, disinformation about Pride Month activities has been plaguing the political and media sphere in Bosnia and Herzegovina, including religious propaganda in Kosovo. The 2022 Belgrade Pride march was particularly targeted, as Serbian far-right political parties and the Serbian Orthodox Church condemned the event and called for a ban via protests that included the glorification of Russian president Vladimir Putin as a model "defender of traditional values."

Libellous claims about the use of the rainbow flag that implicate international institutions, like fake claims about the UN replacing country flags with the flag in Albania, North Macedonia, and Montenegro, and photo montages and AI-generated deepfakes about the Pope spread in Montenegro and North Macedonia, cater to local nationalists. Some local social media influencers plainly parrot Russian narratives about Nazi connections, which is historically ludicrous given that Hitler's regime attempted to exterminate gay people.

Attempts to use an LGBTQ+ connection to emasculate the armies of EU countries and allies, in contrast to supposedly stout Russian armed forces, have been noted in Albania and Montenegro. Stoking the fears of parents is another tactic that affects public opinion in the Western Balkans. In North Macedonia in March, a Coalition for Protection of Children waged a campaign spreading panic about pro-LGBTQ+ indoctrination in schools. The coalition, consisting of 31 small political parties and NGOs, is co-founded by pro-Kremlin fringe political party Rodina Makedonija, with the support of US fundamentalist Christian lobbying organization Family Watch. Defamatory assertions about local schools continue to pop up in Macedonian right-wing media, which sees transphobia as a new key area. Similar manipulations about the use of schools for the indoctrination of children are present in neighbouring Albania.

Other cross-border disinformation trends include promoting stigmatization by connecting sexual orientation with infectious diseases, such as monkeypox, which was seen in Albania, Bosnia, and Herzegovina and used by tabloids and social media trolls in Montenegro, alongside the "classic" association of LGBTQ+ people with paedophilia in Bosnian and Macedonian social network spaces, including lies about the World Economic Forum and EU reactions to discrimination in Hungary. Pride marches and related events taking place in the Balkans during May and June 2023 have been pointing to the devastating effects of homophobia and transphobia, demanding a systemic response to issues of impunity for hate speech and hate crimes that undermine democracy and the rule of law. Such criminal behaviour further erodes the fragile social cohesion of transitional societies, contributing to increasing the already present extreme polarization, as well as normalizing an atmosphere of fear, where any minorities or people with different opinions can be scapegoated.

Not Sure Where to Start?

Write in dialogue a conversation between two versions of yourself: a part of you that feels a moral and ethical responsibility to engage with the issues that lie at the heart of *Disinformation helps weaponize homophobia in the Balkans*; and another part of you that believes you have no business writing about conditions and places that you might not have the lived experience of.

Do not let either part of yourself "win" the debate. Instead, use this intrapersonal dialogue to dig deep into the whys and why-nots of each position.

Text Six

#VoicesOfChange: Residents Unite against Cartels in Guerrero, Mexico

> *This story by Global Voices América Latina (2023)*
> *originally appeared on Global Voices.*

Guerrero is a state on Mexico's Pacific coast, known for its tourist city Acapulco. However, Acapulco is ranked the second most violent city in the world, and Guerrero, the second poorest state in Mexico. Paradoxically, Guerrero also produces the most gold in Mexico, making it a "poisoned treasure" as the increasing dispute between cartels for control of the mining industry unfolds. There are currently 16 organized crime groups operating in Guerrero, the most notorious of which is the organization known as "Los Tlacos," which has made headlines for its threats against politicians. These criminal groups are known for their kidnappings, killings, and control of prices, which in turn have caused people to be displaced. They also deal in crystal meth, an artificially synthesized drug that is extremely addictive and toxic. It currently represents a public health problem in Mexico.

Guerrero is one of the states in which municipal presidents, or incumbent politicians, have been most often accused of having ties to organized crime. The Ministry of National Defence reports that most local governments, in coalition with state and federal government forces, participated in the massacre and disappearance of 43 students in Ayotzinapa. Currently, state governor Evelyn Salgado Pineda has allegedly had compromising ties to the Beltran Leyva Cartel. She is the daughter of Félix Salgado Macedonio, who was also accused in 2021 of having ties to this cartel and to US drug trafficker Edgar Valdez Villarreal, alias "La Barbie," in addition to being accused of sexual violence.

In this context, civil society organizations, communities, or informal groups have emerged to confront up close the problems they live with on a daily basis. One such example is the grassroots organization called "Pueblos Unidos" (United Peoples), which Global Voices interviewed. It has been working for eight years, mainly in the northern area and Tierra Caliente of Guerrero. They previously worked in armed self-defence groups, which are vigilante community groups in Mexico that, faced with the inaction of public authorities, arm to defend themselves from cartel attacks. However, relying on the federal government under an agreement, they have laid down their arms on the condition of getting results. They now dedicate themselves to denouncing the violence and corruption that plagues the region on Facebook, where they have 16,000 followers on their page.

In light of the dangerous situation in Guerrero, criminal threats against Pueblos Unidos, and the ongoing escalation of violence against activists, the interviewee will remain anonymous under the name "Pueblos Unidos" as well as the interviewer, who speaks on behalf of Global Voices. The interview was edited for clarity and is the second instalment of the #VocesDelCambio (#VoicesOfChange) interview series, focused on highlighting the experiences and expertise of human rights activists in Latin America.

Global Voices (GV):	Who is in your group?
Pueblos Unidos (PU):	This organization is made up of many people (both men and women regardless of age), we also have municipal presidents. We are the United Peoples of the Northern Zone and little by little more are joining from the state of Guerrero, because we are tired of seeing our government not doing anything. We became aware towards which criminal group they are closest to, [the criminal group "Los Tlacos."] That's how it is in the whole state. In most of the state, there were self-defence groups years ago, and with the negotiation and the deal they made with [the governor accused of ties to drug trafficking] Felix Salgado Macedonio, they began to destroy the self-defence groups claiming they were responsible for crimes. The Tlacos reached the communities and in the eyes of the federal government, the self-defence groups were criminals.
GV:	Is there any coalition with other organizations or do you work independently?

PU: Not really, Los Tlacos broke the codes
                 between mafias by bringing women
                 and children, that's why we don't allow
                 intermeddling [as the criminal group
                 wanted to infiltrate them].

GV: What led you to take up arms?

PU: Prior to the abuses [committed by
                 organized crime and the government], we
                 have been motivated by the kidnappings
                 that took place previously in the Northern
                 Region of the State of Guerrero. Little by
                 little this led us to take up arms. Today
                 we have laid down our arms and we have
                 handed over security to the state and fed-
                 eral government, but reiterating to them
                 that, if any situation happens within the
                 municipalities of the Northern Zone, we
                 are ready to rise up.

GV: What is your relationship with the state
                 government of Guerrero?

PU: The organization has taken a stand
                 against Evelyn Salgado Pineda, gov-
                 ernor of the state of Guerrero. She is not
                 really the governor, here the mastermind
                 of everything is her father Felix Salgado
                 Macedonio, who took advantage of the
                 Fourth Transformation [the proposed pol-
                 itical change of Mexican President Lopez
                 Obrador and his MORENA party] to put
                 his relatives into this. They have relatives
                 involved in organized crime.

GV: What do you do on a daily basis to
                 fight them?

PU: We opt for social media to spread our
                 needs and hope that someone will listen
                 to us and make us reach the ears of our
                 President of the Republic. The most
                 painful thing here is that we have paisanos
                 [people from the same state or city] with
                 money, [those from Guerrero who are

	businessmen or owners of conglomerates, who have accumulated a great deal of capital]. But we have never been taken into account, when we really needed it. Instead of helping us, they turned their backs on us, and they do have money to spread it through the media at a national level, because they have friends in several important media outlets. Global Voices is the first media that contacted us.
GV:	What encourages you the most to continue fighting despite the threats from organized crime?
PU:	Our young people, they are the ones who really motivate us and what makes us keep on fighting, because we do not want them to try drugs, we have a real battle against crystal meth.
GV:	Have you ever wanted to give up?
PU:	No, not at all, for our families we are willing to give up our lives, even if it is in the hands of the government, or whomever, but the physical integrity of our children and our families is paramount. If the only way out is to pay the price with our lives, we will gladly go, but we want a state free of Tlacos, free of fentanyl and free of crystal meth.

Not Sure Where to Start?

Focus on the interview between GV and PU. Between each of their exchanges, introduce a third voice that represents the kind of outsider *you* are to the issue of violence and resistance in Guerrero. The voice can be a character, a concept, just a voice. For example, if I were to write a response piece by these rules, it might look something like this:

GV: Is there any coalition with other organizations or do
            you work independently?
PU: Not really, Los Tlacos broke the codes between
            mafias by bringing women and children, that's why
            we don't allow intermeddling [as the criminal group
            wanted to infiltrate them].

They say that during the riots, it was the women who were
targeted first. The Hindu women married to Muslim men. The
Muslim women married to Hindu men.

GV: What led you to take up arms?
PU: Prior to the abuses [committed by organized crime
            and the government], we have been motivated by
            the kidnappings that took place previously in the
            Northern Region of the State of Guerrero. Little by
            little this led us to take up arms. Today we have laid
            down our arms and we have handed over security to
            the state and federal government, but reiterating to
            them that, if any situation happens within the munici-
            palities of the Northern Zone, we are ready to rise up.

Maybe we should arm ourselves. Las Mujeres Unidas de la
India. Wouldn't that be something?

    In between every exchange that occurs between the inter-
viewer and Pueblos Unidos, add commentary that places you in
conversation with the ideas being expressed.

Works Cited

Cheikh, S.B. (2023). *Can Algerian human rights defenders be safe in Tunisia?*
    [Online] Global Voices. Available at: https://globalvoices.org/2023/07/28/
    can-algerian-human-rights-defenders-be-safe-in-tunisia/ [Accessed   28
    Aug. 2023].
Global Voices América Latina. (2023). *#VoicesOfChange: Residents unite*
    against cartels in Guerrero, Mexico. [Online] Global Voices. Available
    at: https://globalvoices.org/2023/07/12/voicesofchange-residents-unite-
    against-cartels-in-guerrero-mexico/ [Accessed 28 Aug. 2023].
Global Voices Central & Eastern Europe. (2023). *Disinformation helps*
    weaponize homophobia in the Balkans. [Online] Global Voices. Available
    at: https://globalvoices.org/2023/06/29/disinformation-helps-weaponize-
    homophobia-in-the-balkans/ [Accessed 28 Aug. 2023].

Part Three

Explore Lack of Understanding

Write creative responses to the stories in this section using formal strategies that highlight your distance from the themes and people that the writing addresses. While autoethnography uses the presence of the author's self in the writing to highlight distance from the contexts being discussed, in this approach, you are invited to consider aesthetics that—by their very nature—capture the distance between the writer and the worlds they write about.

How might a formal integration of "gaps" or "lacks" allow a more ethical authorial engagement with experiences of others?

What aspects of a writer's positioning in relation to a context might impact the deployment of such an approach—is there such a thing as an author being so removed from a particular issue or context that their additional use of formal distance presents the others, problematically, as an enigmatic, inexplicable alien (of sorts)?

Are there specific kinds of events or incidences—or degrees of "insider-ness" and "outsider-ness" with regard to the author's lived experience—that might make the use of formal strategies of emotional distancing more or less ethically murky?

DOI: 10.4324/9781032688749-6

Text Seven

"A Great Day to Be a Journalist in Fiji" as Parliament
Repeals "draconian" Media Law

> *This story by Mong Palatino (2023) originally*
> *appeared on Global Voices.*

On 6 April 2023, the Parliament of Fiji voted to repeal the Media Industry Development Act (MIDA) which was enacted in 2010 by the government which had assumed power through a coup in 2006. The new coalition government that was formed after the December 2022 election vowed to pursue reforms in media legislation, which included the review or repeal of the MIDA.

Journalists attended the historic voting at the Parliament. Local journalists and media groups have criticized the MIDA as a repressive tool of the previous government. The statement of the Fijian Media Association (FMA), which was read during the Parliament session, highlighted the deleterious impact of the MIDA on the local media environment. "Some of Fiji's best journalists left the industry as a result," the statement said, "and the media still carry the mental scars today from that very disturbing period." The FMA's statement goes on to mention how "neither the previous government nor a single member of the public has ever used the MIDA Tribunal to complain about the media, and there has been no media development under the MIDA." Calling it "a useless, but dangerous and vindictive piece of legislation for the industry," the FMA says that the "repeal of the MIDA has long been a unifying demand of all media organizations in Fiji. No government, including this People's Coalition government should ever be given such power over the media."

During the session, Minister for Communications, the Hon. Manoa Kamikamica read out the names of journalists who were either harassed or charged by authorities for alleged violations of the MIDA. The FMA added that "the MIDA experiment is over, and the draconian legislation now belongs in the dustbins of history." In an earlier statement, the FMA cited how the repressive provisions of the MIDA undermined media freedom. The excessive fines hanging over the heads of media organisations and editors were threatening, not conducive, to media freedom and designed to be vindictive, and to punish and control the media rather (than) encourage better reporting standards.

After the voting in Parliament, *Fiji Times* editor-in-chief Fred Wesley exclaimed, "Today is a great day to be a journalist in Fiji." He later wrote an editorial linking the MIDA to the decline of democracy in Fiji. "How could you ignore that with massive fines and a jail term hanging over your head daily?" Wesley asked. "Because there was no clear explanation about what constituted a breach, editors faced the very real possibility of someone somewhere using the Act against them."

"It certainly wasn't fashionable standing against the government then," Wesley adds, "raising niggling issues that made those in power look bad. The people do not need absolute control by the government. They don't need suppressed information either." *Islands Business* magazine editor Samantha Magick explained how the repeal of the MIDA will inspire more critical media reporting in Fiji. The country's "media will see more investigations, more depth, more voices, different perspectives, [and] hopefully they can engage a bit more as well without fear," Magick says. "It'll just be so much healthier for us as a people and a democracy to have that level of debate and investigation and questioning, regardless of who you are."

But the previous ruling party said the passage of MIDA was necessary to protect public interest. Former minister Premila Kumar also questioned why legislators consulted the media about the MIDA repeal bill. It is "like going to prison and asking the inmates if bars and gates should be removed," Kumar opines. "Obviously, they will choose to remove anything that is regulating them. Absolute media freedom in any jurisdiction is rare and even impossible."

Alongside Kumar's statement, Deputy Prime Minister Biman Prasad reminded the new opposition about the importance of repealing the MIDA. "Sometimes I think the opposition can't even understand their own interests today," Prasad says. "They are so used to being in government and muzzling the media that they can't see that the repealing of the act will be beneficial for them, good for democracy and good for our people in this country." The Attorney General also assured the opposition and the public that they can still seek redress against abuses through existing laws such as the Defamation Act 1971, the Online Safety Act 2018, and the Crimes Act 2009.

FMA supports media self-regulation through the Fiji Media Council which is composed of media organizations and community representatives to process complaints and improve media standards. The Pacific Islands News Association urged stakeholders to initiate discussions on the self-regulation of the media industry by saying that the "onus is now on the media industry and related stakeholders to put in place proper independent mechanisms for the media to self-regulate and discharge their duties responsibly." It also encouraged other Pacific governments to follow the lead of Fiji by removing restrictive media laws. The 2022 World Press Freedom Index released by Reporters Without Borders placed Fiji in the 102nd position out of 180 countries. It was the worst rating for a Pacific nation.

Not Sure Where to Start?

Describe Fred Wesley's *physical* response in the exact moment that he finds out about the act being repealed. Don't qualify or judge or explain or try to understand. Instead, just explain the physicality in as objective a way as possible.

Is Wesley standing or seated? What are the objects around him? Does he jump in the air, and if so, is his left leg higher up that his right one? Where are his hand, his elbow in relation to the sky? Where do his eyes look? How many crinkles border them?

In the written description of Wesley's physicality in the moment that he finds out about the repeal, focus on the external visual that he creates rather than your interpretation of what might or might not be happening *within* him.

Focus on that which can be described *without* interpretation.

Text Eight

Will Guatemala Face Its Past as It Votes for Its Future?

> *This story by Laura Chaparro Piedrahíta (2023)*
> *originally appeared on Global Voices.*

The year 2023 is, without a doubt, decisive for Guatemala. And, as many wonder what lies ahead for the country, looking to its past is also imperative. The general presidential elections are due to be held on 25 June, and polls show a high level of pessimism among Guatemalans. The context for this is severe human rights violations, the curtailed state of press freedom, violent deaths because of organized crime, excessive use of force by the military and private security agents, and the exclusion of three candidates from the electoral race. More critically, none of the presidential candidates has included the implementation of the Agreement for a Firm and Lasting Peace signed between the State and the guerrillas represented by the Guatemalan National Revolutionary Unit in 1996, nor the transitional justice process that has been underway in the country for more than a decade.

In order to move into the future, the country must first resolve its past. Between 1990 and 1996, Guatemala was immersed in an internal armed conflict that brought gruesome human rights violations to thousands of victims, primarily peasants, members of Indigenous communities, and women. In the context of the Cold War disputes, the Mayan peoples became internal enemies of the State, being internally displaced in a framework of violence and disproportionate use of state force. This led to multiple cases of arbitrary executions, enforced disappearances, and excessive use of violence against women, most of them happening during the dictatorships of General Romeo Lucas García and Efraín Ríos Montt. Subsequently, a critical transitional justice process was established in 1996 to investigate the abuses committed during that time, provide reparations to the victims, and prosecute those responsible for such atrocities.

Nevertheless, in the last five years, on three different occasions, new legislation has been discussed. These initiatives seek to prohibit the prosecution of members of the army, state security forces, and members of the insurgent groups, in addition to releasing people who were convicted or are facing criminal proceedings for any act committed during the armed conflict. If approved, this legislation would represent a drastic setback for survivors, victims, and their relatives. The press and human rights advocates have called it an "amnesty law."

Transitional Justice Is Crucial to Peacebuilding

The case of Guatemala is one of many illustrating the complexity of transitional justice in Latin America, a pioneer continent in the application of such approaches aimed at responding to the legacies of massive human rights violations through the establishment of truth commissions, the granting of reparations to the victims, and, in many cases, judicial proceedings against the perpetrators. According to the

United Nations, transitional justice covers the full range of processes and mechanisms associated with a society's attempt to come to terms with a legacy of large-scale past conflict, repression, violations, and abuses to ensure accountability, serve justice and achieve reconciliation through four fundamental pillars: truth, justice, reparation, and measures of non-recurrence, with a primary focus on recognizing the dignity and fulfilling the rights of the victims.

The first countries to implement transitional justice models in the region were Argentina in 1984 and Chile in 1990, two nations that suffered the impact of military dictatorships. Afterwards, Peru began a transition period by mitigating a systematic campaign of abuses under an emergency law enacted a few years later. Colombia was the latest country to sign an ambitious General Agreement for the Termination of the Conflict and the Construction of a Stable and Lasting Peace in 2016, ending the continent's oldest internal armed conflict. Thus, transitional justice is fundamental to advancing peacebuilding, as it points the way toward a democratic society in which citizens are treated with dignity.

Amnesty Laws Jeopardize Guatemala's Transitional Justice Advancements

Initiatives that seek to approve amnesty laws promote impunity, deny the rights of those who have suffered the consequences of the conflict, seriously undermine efforts to advance peacebuilding and recognition of the truth, and ignore the complexity of the armed conflict and abuses committed against local communities. Guatemala has made substantial progress, such as establishing the National Reparations Program created in 2003 to compensate the victims. Regarding truth-seeking initiatives, the report of the Commission on Historical Clarification (CEH) set up to clarify the facts and circumstances surrounding the armed confrontations, in its 1999 report "Guatemala: Memory of silence," has given an account of the atrocities perpetrated during the decades of war that left more than 200,000 people affected. The report issued a series of recommendations (one of them, precisely, on the lack of truth mechanisms and proper investigations of the crimes and wrongdoers) to make the four pillars of transitional justice more accessible, although at present only a few have been fully implemented.

Likewise, the Inter-American Court of Human Rights has reiterated in various rulings that the lack of investigation, prosecution, and punishment of those responsible for gross human rights violations contributes to impunity and limits reparations for the damages caused. To date, the Court has issued 29 judgments in cases involving human rights violations in Guatemala, 15 of which for cases that took place during the internal armed conflict. Besides, the court has even granted precautionary measures to the victims, ordering the State to suspend the processing of the reform of the National Reconciliation Law, a proposal that is still in Congress pending approval.

Human rights experts, international civil society organizations, victims' organizations, and survivors of the warfare have reiterated the risks to be derived from the possible approval of this amnesty law. On the one hand, it poses a significant obstacle to the progress achieved in the fight against impunity for human rights breaches, and especially for the evolution of transitional justice, accountability, and the necessary construction of historical memory, as it would contribute to the repetition of these aggressions and would promote a cycle of violence and despotism in the country. The lack of investigation and prosecution of these atrocious acts would also violate international human rights law principles. Finally, it would greatly hinder Guatemala's justice system and the rule of law.

A Challenge and an Opportunity

The upcoming elections represent an enormous challenge for transitional justice in Guatemala but also a noteworthy opportunity to make visible the magnitude and gravity of the violence, as well as to draw attention to the importance of state intervention to ensure that the outrages committed in the context of the armed conflict are not repeated. Therefore, the development of concrete public policies aimed at ratifying the State's responsibility in administering justice and creating government programs primarily targeting those who need them most are key. Once elected, the new president must reiterate the commitment to implement, without further delay, the peace accords, intensify the work of the truth commission in search of missing persons, make reparations to the victims, and ensure the events that fomented the atrocities of the war do not ever occur again, and that the structural problems that gave rise to the conflict, including racism, inequalities, and lack of political participation, do not contribute to the longed-for peace and become a distant dream.

Not Sure Where to Start?

Write a series of three vignettes that are *non*-verbal images accompanied by light and sound.

In the first vignette, use words to extensively describe a still image—a photograph or a sculpture—of a historical event from Guatemala's past. Describe the placement of bodies or objects in a specific composition, accompanied by a particular kind of light and sound; perhaps a multimedia photograph or a multisensorial sculpture. Then, within this vignette, build an aesthetic strategy that captures the distance of your understanding. You could include the character of a sculptor who arranges and rearranges the bodies or objects because they are unable to arrive at a configuration that seems sufficiently representative.

In the next multisensorial sculpture, describe how those same bodies and objects and lights and sounds morph (or not) in that past event's manifestation in the country's present. Then, within that vignette, build a different aesthetic that embodies the distance of your understanding. Perhaps the discords in the vignette are captured through sound: words and phrases in languages that are *not* spoken in Guatemala.

In the final vignette, use words to describe a multimedia photograph of Guatemala's future. Like the ones that came before it, build in an aesthetic that embodies the degrees of your "insider/outsider-ness." How can you use the integration of light and darkness to highlight or obscure aspects of your image and, in so doing, capture the gaps in your understanding?

Text Nine

Hong Kong Court Asks: Who Are the Defendants of the Protest Anthem Injunctions?

> *This story by Oiwan Lam (2023) originally appeared on Global Voices.*

Hong Kong's High Court adjourned to 21 July 2023 an injunction hearing on the government's request to ban the distribution of the protest anthem "Glory to Hong Kong." Judge Wilson Chan Ka-shun asked the Department of Justice (DoJ) to clarify the definition of the defendant in a hearing of the government's injunction application on June 12. While the DoJ stressed in the court that the injunctions did not intend to target "the world at large," the scope of the prohibition application is extensive and vague. In the DoJ's writ, the defendant is written as "persons conducting themselves in any of the acts prohibited under paragraph 1(a), (b), (c) or (d) of the indorsement of claim."

The indorsement of claim cites the National Security Law (NSL), Sedition Law, and National Anthem Ordinance as the legal base for the injunctions, which seek to restrain anyone from broadcasting, performing, printing, publishing, selling, offering for sale, distributing, disseminating, displaying, or reproducing the protest song in any media form, including on the internet (a) with inciting secession or sedition intentions; and (b) to mislead others into taking the song as Hong Kong's national anthem or to insult the national anthem. Moreover, the claim also covers acts that (c) assist, cause, procure, incite, aid, abet others, or (d) knowingly authorize, permit or allow others to commit the prohibited acts are also covered by the injunction order.

Who Will Defend against the Injunction Application?

Since the injunctions sought to restrain everyone in Hong Kong, the judge was concerned about how the DoJ could deliver the legal document to the defendant, thereby postponing the hearing so that the public could prepare for the defence. The Hong Kong government made a similar injunction attempt during the 2019 protests to prohibit anyone from posting and reposting any information that promotes violence on online platforms, including LIHKG and Telegram. It also targeted any party who "aids" or "abets" others to commit unlawful acts. Back then, the Hong Kong Internet Society crowdfunded a judicial review because the injunction would undermine the city's free flow of information as it anticipated that the government might use the injunction to force online platforms and ISPs to censor and restrict access to websites and applications, or request private information of online users who are aiding the dissemination of the content. In the current case, the high court judge has given more time for the public to prepare for the defence; yet, after years of crackdowns on NGOs and crowdfunding activities, it is unlikely that any remaining civic group can stand up to defend the anthem in the court's hearing.

Who Are the Defendants: Google or Local ISPs?

The question regarding who the defendants are has lingered among concerned citizens since the DoJ filed the injunction. As stated in the government press release, the motivation for the injunction application is related to the recent national anthem mix-up and chaos in international events. The "Song has also been mistakenly presented as the 'national anthem of Hong Kong' (instead of the correct one 'March of the Volunteers') repeatedly." According to the press release, this "mistake has not only insulted the national anthem but also caused serious damage to the country and the HKSAR."

Both the Hong Kong government and pro-Beijing politicians have blamed Google, the major search engine, for "misleading" search results and causing confusion after the tech giant refused to manipulate the search result. Hence, many believe that the injunction is targeting Google. In 2022, the Hong Kong government requested Google remove 330 content items, among which 57 were related to national security. The company complied with about half of the requests. Although the lyrics of the protest song "Glory to Hong Kong" contain the slogan "Liberate Hong Kong, revolution of our times," which was interpreted as inciting secession given the context of the protest in a court trial, the song is not illegal. The injunctions, once granted, may be cited as legal grounds for content removal requests. In the writ, the DoJ attached a list of 32 YouTube videos, which are different versions of the protest song. However, whether the Google office in Hong Kong will comply with the injunctions is still a question, as the tech company is registered in the US, which is outside the reach of the injunction order's jurisdiction, as pointed out by Tse Lin Chung, a Hong Kong lawyer: Since YouTube is based in the US, the court summons must be delivered to their headquarters to ask the companies to attend the hearing. "Even if [the injunction] successfully restrained Google," Chung states, " it would only prohibit its circulation within Hong Kong." This is because, Chung explains, the "SAR government has to apply an injunction in the US in order to take down the videos globally" and the "US court would not approve such an injunction." Since the "Google office in Hong Kong is not responsible for the operation of YouTube," Chung offers the opinion that "the local court could not ask Google staffers to implement the injunction and punish them as if they represented the headquarter." While the injunction may force Google to block the song locally, it cannot force Google to take down the related videos globally.

Meanwhile, local ISPs are worried that if YouTube or other platforms do not comply with the injunctions once granted by the court, they will have to block these platforms from local access.

As explained by Lento Yip Yuk Fai, chairman of the Hong Kong Internet Service Providers Association, the injunction, once granted, would penalise anyone for "assisting," "causing," "aiding," or "knowingly allowing" others to disseminate the protest song. As data flow on the internet is encrypted, they can't block local users from accessing specific content. If they are required to comply with the injunction fully, they may have to block entire platforms where different versions of the song are hosted and shared. ISPs in Hong Kong have blocked local users' access to certain websites, such as the UK-based Hong Kong Watch, since the NSL was enacted in 2020. Given that the injunction cannot apply globally, it would not stop the protest song from appearing at the top of the search result when searching "Hong Kong national anthem" on search engines outside Hong Kong—Tse Lin Chung anticipated the injunction would merely ban performances of the song in the streets.

After the protest slogan "Liberate Hong Kong, revolution of our times" was ruled as inciting secession in court, singing "Glory to Hong Kong" in street performance has become an invitation for police attention or even arrest without injunctions. On the other hand, the government's legal gesture has boosted the popularity of the song again […] For about one week since the DoJ filed the injunction application, "Glory to Hong Kong" dominated the local iTunes top 10. On 14 June, the protest anthem vanished from major music streaming sites in Hong Kong, including Spotify and Apple.

Not Sure Where to Start?

Identify the two most directly oppositional stakeholders: the proponents of the anthem that is being banned and the authorities banning it. Craft headlines or phrases that capture each of these different stakeholders' points of view and place them side by side, without giving one weight over the other.

HEADLINE 1 FROM GROUP 1	HEADLINE 1 FROM GROUP 2
HEADLINE 2 FROM GROUP 1	HEADLINE 2 FROM GROUP 2
HEADLINE 3 FROM GROUP 1	HEADLINE 3 FROM GROUP 2

A note of caution with this strategy: while the approach of offering viewpoints from oppositional voices can capture the distance of a writer from the issue or context being examined—i.e., the outsider does not know enough to pick a side—this aesthetic should be accompanied by some serious considerations: to what extent does *not* giving weight to one ideology or side contain the risk of giving the oppressors' voices as much importance as those of their oppressed? Can any degree of an author's "outsider-ness" with regard to the story being told justify *not* taking a stand against what—to some, to many, to you, to me—might be an obvious violation of a human's rights?

Works Cited

Lam, O. (2023). *Hong Kong Court asks: Who are the defendants of the protest anthem injunctions?* [Online] Global Voices. Available at: https://globalvoices.org/2023/06/15/hong-kong-court-asks-who-are-the-defendants-of-the-protest-anthem-injunctions/ [Accessed 28 Aug. 2023].

Palatino, M. (2023). *"A great day to be a journalist in Fiji" as Parliament repeals "draconian" media law.* [Online] Global Voices. Available at: https://globalvoices.org/2023/04/09/a-great-day-to-be-a-journalist-in-fiji-as-parliament-repeals-draconian-media-law/ [Accessed 28 Aug. 2023].

Piedrahíta, L.C. (2023). *Will Guatemala face its past as it votes for its future?* [Online] Global Voices. Available at: https://globalvoices.org/2023/06/22/will-guatemala-face-its-past-as-it-votes-for-its-future/ [Accessed 28 Aug. 2023].

Part Four

Explore Visual Aesthetics

Explore visual aesthetics—layout, typography—when crafting written responses to the news stories that follow. What might this look like?

A more expected aesthetic
I am going to tell you, the reader, how I navigate my own positioning when I write about what is happening in Ukraine in 2023.

One that tries to perform its being an outsider to the setting:

> Ukraine   still   crumbles
>   likebutnotlike   streets
>   in San
> Francisco.

How can considerations of visual aesthetic augment the experience of writing and reading stories written by others about others?

How can outsider-writers explore the use of font and space and shape on the page so that the push-pull they navigate when writing about others might take on additional dimensions?

When we choose to push the limits of form and explore not only what our words but also how they appear on the page, how do we navigate the risk that our experimentation might make the other's story inaccessible?

DOI: 10.4324/9781032688749-7

> Are there specific kinds of events or incidences—or degrees of "insider-ness" and "outsider-ness" with regard to the author's lived experience—that make the use of a textual, visual aesthetic experimentation more or less ethically murky?

Text Ten

Reviving the Cree and Ojibwe Languages of Manitoba with TikTok

> *This story by Rising Voices (2021) originally appeared on Global Voices.*

As a child growing up in the Fox Lake Cree Nation in Northern Manitoba, Canada, Sharissa Neault would hear the Ininímowin (Cree) language from her grandparents. However, the language was not passed on to her mother and consequently not to Neault either.

"As I grew older, I heard less and less Ininímowin until I believed it was lost," she would recount in an email interview with Rising Voices. Fast forward to the present day, and Neault has moved to Winnipeg and has started working at the Manitoba Indigenous Cultural Education Centre (MICEC), a non-profit educational organization that provides programs and services to help raise awareness of Indigenous cultures in the Province of Manitoba. This Canadian Province is located in Cree, Dakota, Dene, Ojibway, and Oji-Cree traditional First Nations territories, and the Métis Nation.

After she began working at the MICEC, Neault saw diverse ways to promote these languages, including social media. She joined forces with Noah Malazdrewicz, who was actively involved with sharing the Ojibwe language, and they begin creating TikTok videos on the Centre's account. Combining humour, everyday language use, and relatable situations, these videos contribute to making the language accessible, especially during the pandemic when many people were at home. The results have been gratifying, as Neault shared with the News Site of the University of Winnipeg, where she is currently studying: "Young people are seeing it and saying, 'Thank you, I heard my granny say this as a kid,' 'I haven't heard my language in years, thank you,' or 'I didn't know I could still learn my language,'" Neault said. "The comments make it worth it."

In this short interview with Rising Voices, she shares further information about herself, her language, and her digital activism:

Rising Voices (RV):	What is the current status of your language both offline and on the internet?
Sharissa Neault (SN):	There are 5 dialects of the Cree language, which also vary by community. My family speaks the n dialect (Swampy Cree), and my community's dialect of Cree will die in the next 10–20 years with our last remaining fluent speakers. In other communities across Manitoba, I would estimate that there are fewer than 500 fluent speakers under 50. When our older fluent speakers pass, we will rely on these few young people, and their children to carry the language both online and offline. The n dialect is lacking in language learning resources, however, there are people who are working hard to create them alongside our remaining fluent speakers. The y dialect (Plains Cree) is in much better shape, with a higher number of speakers under 50, and many more online and offline resources.
RV:	What have been the biggest challenges for you during your activities to promote your language and culture on the internet? And what are some of the ways that you have been trying to overcome these challenges?
SN:	My biggest challenge has been finding the time to create content with other work commitments. I do my best to create content when I can, and in the past have created a collection of videos to post when I cannot record regularly.
RV:	What are your main motivations for your language digital activism?
SN:	My main motivations are the Indigenous youth who are just like me when I was 15. The Indigenous youth who think their culture and language are lost. I hope that

RV: when they see us, and hear us, they can see and hear themselves; I hope I can help at least one person who is like me, to pick up their language again.

RV: What are your hopes and dreams for your language?

SN: I hope that Ininímowin stays with us long enough for my grandchildren, or my great grandchildren, or my great-great grandchildren and so on, to learn the language as their first language, and understand the complex culture that is embedded in every word. That is all I hope for.

Not Sure Where to Start?

Use the same text as in the article, changing only the *size* of the fonts that are used and explore how such visual shifts might reveal new dynamics in what Sharissa Neault already articulates. For example, let's take the first paragraph and reimagine it using a play with font size:

"As a child growing up in the Fox Lake Cree Nation in Northern Manitoba, Canada, Sharissa Neault would hear the Ininímowin (Cree) language from her grandparents"

"However, the language was not passed on to her mother and consequently not to Neault either"

"As I grew older"

"I heard less and less Ininimowin until"

"I believed it was lost."

Text Eleven

In Azerbaijan, Feminist Activists Say Not the Time to Celebrate

*This story by Arzu Geybullayeva (2023)
originally appeared on Global Voices.*

Three women, with a hand drawn over their throats, staged a flash mob on the premises of the US Embassy in Azerbaijan's capital Baku during the Fourth of July celebrations hosted by the embassy. All three were eventually escorted out of the embassy and a journalist covering the flash mob was handed over to the local police with his hands twisted behind his back as if he were a criminal. The activists saw the event as an opportunity to remind the guests that the time, while village residents were being silenced, the media was being censored, and rights abuses were rampant in Azerbaijan, was not right for drinking wine and celebrating. All four were taken to one of the local police stations, from where they were released after questioning. According to Sanubar Heydarova, one of the activists who took part in the flash mob, "When they were taking us away, the Ambassador was standing right next to us. When I called his name, he looked the other way."

In a statement to Azerbaijan Service for Radio Liberty, the embassy said, "The US Embassy supports fundamental freedoms, including freedom of protest and expression" and that "only some parts of the official program were open to the media. The main part was to network, share the diversity of the United States and celebrate the official event." No further remarks were made about the way the activists and journalist Ulvi Hasanli were escorted or treated. "In Azerbaijan rights are being violated. [The state and the police] are holding people by their throats," said Heydarova as she removed the scarf covering her throat as the three activists entered the premises of the embassy. Gulnara Mehdiyeva, who too took part in the flash mob said, "today both opposition and state representatives have gathered here to celebrate the independence of another country. Meanwhile in Azerbaijan independence is completely suffocated, the voices of media and the people are suffocated, activists are arrested and tortured, and this is how we are protesting the current environment in a civilized manner." "No member of the parliament or a minister have spoken about the torture and rights violations of residents of Söyüdlü village. So, they have time to come here but no time to make statements about their own country," said third activist, Narmin Shahmarzade.

Hasanli later wrote, "Embassy security twisted my arms after I started filming the activists staging the flash mob and handed me over to the local police. I did not expect such violent behaviour on the territory of the embassy. This was an interference with my journalistic activities. Also, I did not expect that the peacefully protesting feminists—Narmin Shahmarzade, Gulnara Mehdiyeva and Sanubar Heydarova—would be handed over to the police. This is a shameful incident. This time I was worried about the US Embassy. The embassy of a country that talks about democracy and human rights and freedom of the press should not have behaved in this way." In an interview with the Ismail Djalilov, host of the YouTube show "Let's talk straight" Hasanli said all of four were treated as if they were terrorists or had committed a crime. "A representative of the press office approached me as I started filming the activists," Haslani describes, "telling me, that I did not have a permission to film here and asked whether I had an accreditation"—although she had "already filmed the speeches of the Ambassador, the garden of the embassy where the reception was held." Haslani further questions the action by agreeing that if indeed "filming the flash mob [was] problematic," the authorities could have "simply asked us to leave. It was shameful that instead they handed us over to Azerbaijani police, the very same structure the US State Department is critical of. This was shameful and they should apologize" said Hasanli. Gulnara Mehdiyeva later wrote on Facebook that the women staged the flash mob after the formal part of the reception was over. "We took off our scarves in front of the local authorities during the informal part of the event and spoke to Ulvi Hasanli on camera. For those who are talking about ethics," Mehdiyeva says, "the biggest unethical thing is to happily celebrate someone else's independence against the background of oppression and brutality happening in the country."

On its official Facebook page, the embassy wrote, "The annual reception celebrated American road trips and showcased both the diversity of the American cultural landscape and the vibrant, multi-faceted cooperation between the United States and Azerbaijan." At least ten political activists left the embassy premises following the extraction of feminist activists and Hasanli.

Protests in Söyüdlü

Since June 20, residents of Söyüdlü village, located in the Gadabay district in western Azerbaijan, have been protesting the environmental damage caused as a result of gold mining in the village and objecting to the construction plans for a second artificial lake. Residents say the existing artificial lake, built in 2012, is used to dump toxic waste from the mine, according to reporting by Meydan TV and OC Media. The waste is poisoning the drinking water with severe consequences on residents' health. The protests quickly escalated because of disproportionate state response, with reports of several residents arrested and fined, journalists battered, and civic activists critical of the state response to the protests facing detention in the capital Baku. On 22 June, police installed checkpoints for entry into the village, verifying address registrations of anyone trying to enter the village. At least one resident has been missing for four days, according to reporting by Meydan TV, and police arrested two men, who recently returned from Russia, for having created a WhatsApp group. Residents say the group was created during the pandemic, and the two men came to attend a funeral. Another resident, who printed the posters held by the village residents, was also reportedly detained and is facing drug possession charges. One of the detained activists is former political prisoner Giyas Ibrahimov. He has been sentenced to 30 days in administrative detention on bogus charges of resisting police. On 24 June, new charges were levelled against the activist, this time accusing Ibrahimov of spreading prohibited information on the internet.

Not Sure Where To Start?

Pick voices that, in your opinion, capture different perspectives from the incident in the article above. How could you use the spatial layout on the page to capture the dynamics of what is being expressed?

What if the narrative from the perspective of the protester was written on the left side of the page?

What if the narrative from the perspective of the protester was written on the right side of the page?

What if the only text that is placed in between is your commentary as an author who lies outside the very specific borders of the event that is being discussed?

What is gained and lost with such a spatial exploration?

Text Twelve

Burundian Women Reclaim Self-worth Thanks to Their Resilience

This story by Ibihé (2023) originally
appeared on Global Voices.

Amida Uwingabiye's story is sadly not uncommon for Burundian women: she was thrown out of her home and abused by her husband for giving birth to a girl. She subsequently lived in poverty from 2003 to 2009. According to the Demographic and Health Survey in Burundi (EDSB III), published by the National Institute of Statistics of Burundi (INSBU) in 2019, around 36 percent of Burundian women experienced physical violence between 2016 and 2017. In fact, while 10 percent of women reported physical violence during pregnancy, 23 percent also reported sexual violence. Didace Ndayikengurukiye, a researcher in family sociology, explains the origins of gender-based violence in Burundi. "Gender-based violence is rooted in Burundian culture," Ndayikengurukiye states. "As we're part of a patriarchal system, societal norms favour men whilst subtly discriminating against women. One acts superior to the other. This behaviour is common amongst uneducated individuals in rural areas." This survey (EDSB III) appears to confirm the influence of educational backgrounds on gender-based violence: "Men and women in the wealthiest quintile, with at least a secondary education, are both less likely to be victims of physical and domestic abuse."

How Amida Overcame Gender-based Violence (GBV)

As a victim of psychological trauma, Amida had lost all confidence before launching her own association in 2009 to address another major issue: poverty amongst homeless women. Between 2016 and 2017, the poverty rate for Burundi's divorced, separated, and widowed women increased to 76.8 percent, while this rate for married women increased to 56.5 percent over the same period. With an average annual income of 186 euros (USD 202), Burundi is one of the poorest countries in the world. More than half of the country's population, 51.4 percent, live below the poverty line. Thanks to the support of Janvière Nibaruta, a moderator for the Nawe Nuze (Come with Us) Care International Initiative, Amida founded the association "Garukira abakenyezi bahukanye n'inkumi zavyariye iwabo" (Standing by Divorced and Unmarried Women). This association brings together women from Masasu Hill in the Gasorwe commune of the country's north-eastern Muyinga Province. She proudly recalls how "three months after the savings bank began operating in 2009, I secured a loan of BIF 15,000 (USD 5.3) from this cooperative to begin selling vegetables on Gasorwe market. I was successful thanks to this loan. In just four months, I had gone from BIF 15,000 to BIF 400,000 (USD 140)."

Amida Constantly Reinvents Herself

However, after becoming quickly disillusioned by her customers not paying the correct prices, Amida changed focus and started selling women's clothing and shoes instead. Over time, a fellow trader introduced her to the Kampala market in Uganda to find items to sell. With a capital of just BIF 800,000 (USD 281.69), she managed to make a profit that saw her capital double in just a week. That said, she notes the difficulty she had in speaking English in this Ugandan market. "To stock up in Uganda's capital city of Kampala, I would tap on the item I wanted to buy and show the vendor the price I wanted to pay on my calculator," Amida shares. "My ability to negotiate with my clothing suppliers was pretty limited since I communicated like a deaf person. However, I got used to it even so."

Fraud at Its Peak

In 2014, when cases of fraud were spiking in Muyinga, one of the country's 18 provinces, Amida was found to be working illegally by the Burundi Revenue Authority (OBR). She explains how at "that time, OBR caught me off guard by seizing my goods worth BIF 7,000,000 (USD 2,464) and selling them at auction when I had committed fraud." Amida now appreciates the importance of associations like the Burundi Association of Business Women (AFAB) and the Burundi Cross Border Traders Association (ACTF), which educate traders in the practice of legal trading by complying with taxation laws and regulations. What's more, she calls upon these organizations to inten-sify their efforts and further educate business owners in this area. In 2016, Amida received business management and financial education training from Young Entrepreneurs' Park (PARJE). She also won a competition as part of the "Campagne Narateye Intambwe" (I Stepped

Up) project on saving and borrowing. For three months, she travelled across the country, using her experience as a lesson for other women.

Mobile Restaurant

However, her journey doesn't end there. She describes that "upon returning from my triumphant business trip, my blood brother, who had my full confidence and even had access to my bank accounts in my absence, had stolen BIF 20,000,000 from me, which is around USD 7,040 (…) I trusted him, and he betrayed me." She sought to get back on her feet despite suffering this painful blow. No longer able to continue with her business, she moved on to mobile food services instead. Due to a lack of appropriate equipment, she sold her car to buy kitchen utensils for her new business. Today, Amida can feed 150 people per day. In a business with a capital of BIF 1,000,000 (USD 352), she employs more than 20 individuals when she receives event orders. Amida is also involved in the trading of foodstuffs, like rice and beans in Kobero, a border town on the border with Tanzania. As she is in high demand and thereby unable to accommodate all her customers, she took out a two-year loan of BIF 7,500,000 (USD 2,640) with the Burundian NGO, Union of Cooperation and Development (UCODE), which she will pay back in regular monthly instalments.

Challenges of Getting a Loan as a Woman

Amida, the owner of a home mortgaged at more than BIF 30,000,000 (USD 10,563), says she had applied for a loan of over BIF 7,500,000 (USD 2,640). UCODE eventually granted her BIF 7,500,000. Data from the Bank of the Republic of Burundi is consistent with Amida's testimony. According to the latest report on the range of formal financial products and services available in Burundi, which was conducted in 2016 and published in 2017, women had less access to loans than men, both as individual customers and associations. Over the space of three years, women saw a fall in their access to loans as individuals. The number of women gaining access to loans dropped from 141,970 in 2014 to 81,558 in 2016. This is a fall of 57.4 percent. However, men saw an increase in their access to loans as individuals over this same period. The number of men gaining access to loans thereby increased from 214,346 to 317,126, which is an increase of 67.6 percent over this three-year period. For Amida, getting a bank loan as a business-woman is a real struggle. "Although I had submitted all the necessary information, I had been asking for this loan for more than two years to no avail." Amida explains that "bankers reluctantly grant women loans. They don't take women's requests for loans seriously. It took the intervention of a Care International employee, who listened to my testimony, to get this loan."

Not Sure Where to Start?

Is there a way to tell Amida's story only through numbers? Which numbers would capture her success? Which numbers would have to surround hers to highlight their relative significance amidst the other numbers in that region? How might these different numbers be laid out on the page to most effectively capture Amida's journey: would they be in different fonts, perhaps, or in different numbering systems entirely?

Consider the use of the serial sevens in Sarah Kane's (2015) *4.48 Psychosis* where the layout of the numbers is used to capture the shifting mental state of the character(s). While one iteration appears like this (Kane, 2001, p. 5),

100
93
86
79
72
65
58
51
44
37
30
23
16
9
2

Another version of Kane's list (2001, p. 6) appears like this:

100

91

84

81

72   69

58

44

37   38

42

21   28

12

7

Works Cited

Geybullayeva, A. (2023). *In Azerbaijan, feminist activists say not the time to celebrate*. [Online] Global Voices. Available at: https://globalvoices.org/2023/06/28/in-azerbaijan-feminist-activists-say-not-the-time-to-celebrate/ [Accessed 28 Aug. 2023].

Ibihé. (2023). *Burundian women reclaim self-worth thanks to their resilience*. [Online] Global Voices. Available at: https://globalvoices.org/2023/07/17/burundian-women-reclaim-self-worth-thanks-to-their-resilience/ [Accessed 28 Aug. 2023].

Kane, S. (2001). *4.48 Psychosis*. London: Metheun Drama.

Rising Voices. (2021). *Global Voices—Reviving the Cree and Ojibwe languages of Manitoba with TikTok*. [Online] Global Voices. Available at: https://globalvoices.org/2021/09/25/reviving-the-cree-and-ojibwe-languages-of-manitoba-with-tiktok/ [Accessed 28 Aug. 2023].

Part Five

Explore Banalities

Explore, in your written response to the three news stories that follow, a more banal, ordinary aspect in the lives it describes. Stay away from centring the spectacular event: the war, or the earthquake, or the devastating account of a condition or event or phenomenon that you have not lived. Instead, approach the place, the people or the context through the lens of the quotidian, the everyday, the prosaic.

What happens when, as writers, we focus *not* on the qualities of another's life that are radically different from our own, but instead, on actions and activities and daily rituals that might even resemble our own?

How might an exploration of the intensely *ordinary*, in a setting that is defined by its distance from our own reality, be employed to allow a more ethical artistic approach—while also calibrating against oversimplification?

Are there some levels of "outsider-ness" to which there is no banal, where even the seemingly smallest action in someone else's life presents something that's out of the ordinary? What are those levels of otherness, for you?

DOI: 10.4324/9781032688749-8

Text Thirteen

*Fish Are Poured into Jamaica's Rio Cobre after Pollution
Incidents, But Is This the End of the Matter?*

> *This story by Emma Lewis (2023) originally
> appeared on Global Voices.*

In the "Land of Wood and Water" ("Xaymaca," the island's Taino
name) residents are justly proud of their beautiful rivers and waterfalls.
Dunn's River Falls is listed as Jamaica's top tourist attraction and
there are some beautiful riverside spots that are popular with local
Jamaicans. However, Jamaica's rivers face unprecedented challenges.
These include severe and prolonged droughts, resulting from climate change. The river feeding Somerset Falls, a popular waterfall
attraction has run dry, and it was closed. Although rivers sometimes
disappear underground during the dry season, the attraction's man-
ager said the closure was due to the absence of the expected rainy
season in April. Human activities affecting rivers include deforest-
ation, extractive industries such as sand mining (legal and illegal),
the dumping of garbage, and even the reported poisoning of a river
in eastern Jamaica by residents wanting to catch fish—also not a new
phenomenon.

One of the most long-suffering in recent years is the island's second-
longest river, the Rio Cobre. In 2019, 2021, and again in 2022, the
river allegedly received overflows of effluent from the nearby bauxite
plant operated by the West Indies Alumina Company (WINDALCO)
and owned by UC Rusal. The governmental National Environment
and Planning Agency (NEPA) reported that WINDALCO had "lost
sight of its processes" during the 2022 pollution and that the company
would be held accountable and prosecuted. NEPA currently has three
cases against WINDALCO pending in court (from 2019, 2021, and
2022). On each occasion, the pollution from the company's holding
ponds resulted in major fish kills and loss of livelihoods for communities depending on the river, besides the continued degradation of
the riverine environment. In January 2023, WINDALCO began the
construction of a new effluent pond, with the intention of preventing
further overflows. After the 2022 spillage, NEPA's CEO observed that
the company had been "given enough time to comply with the terms

and conditions of its operating environmental permits and environmental licences."

On 30 June this year, WINDALCO began restocking the river with fish, with advice from Jamaica's Fisheries Division and guidance from an unnamed independent environmental consultant hired by WINDALCO. It is not clear whether the operation was guided by this assessment, notes the non-governmental organisation Jamaica Environment Trust (JET), which monitors the situation along with another Jamaican NGO, Freedom Imaginaries and the community-based Friends of the Rio Cobre. JET immediately issued a press release and raised concerns over the way the restocking exercise was done. Both JET and the community said they were not informed in advance and residents were surprised by the appearance of men with buckets of fish. A total of 4,000 tilapia fingerlings were deposited in the river. It was alleged that some of the fish had subsequently died, but this was not confirmed. JET also asserted that the restocking, which is to be done in four phases, according to WINDALCO, was done without briefing the fishers on the type of fish to be introduced, or any other relevant information. A lack of transparency in the matter remains a major concern. Despite several letters sent to NEPA requesting a copy of the ecological assessment report, JET says it has not received it.

So, what is the current situation? There have been no updates since the 30 June activity, and it is not known when or where the restocking will continue. Civil society organisations are seeking a meeting with officials. CEO of JET Theresa Rodriguez-Moodie noted via text to Global Voices: "Following the start of the restocking of the Rio Cobre, JET, Friends of Rio Cobre, Freedom Imaginaries, and Jamaicans for Justice reached out to NEPA requesting an urgent meeting with themselves and representatives from the National Fisheries Authority (NFA), the Jamaica Bauxite Institute (JBI), and any other relevant agency." Rodriguez-Moodie elaborates that the "primary objective of this meeting was for us to gain a better understanding of the plans with respect to the restocking of the Rio Cobre." Although the "request was acknowledged but the date proposed to meet was not suitable and NEPA was to suggest a new date." Rodriguez-Moodie says that "JET followed up on 13 July but we have had no response since." JET founder and environmental activist Diana McCaulay focused on the concerning question of the fish species itself. Tilapia is a non-native, invasive species. Native species would include perch, crayfish, shrimp, mullet, and dog tooth fish. In her column headlined "Who speaks for the river?" McCaulay observed that "undoubtedly, restocking the Rio Cobre with a species common in Jamaican rivers is best for the fishers. But where is the voice of the agency set up to speak for the river itself—the National Environment and Planning Agency (NEPA)?"

The various species of Tilapia brought into Jamaica are native to Africa, and they are a well-documented invasive species in other parts of the world. Here, as in many places, even where they were not deliberately introduced to rivers, they escaped to rivers and streams from fishponds, and soon native species were extremely rare. Nor are Tilapia the only invasive species to be found in our rivers. We also have Australian red claw and catfish and, perhaps, many others. Why should we care? Simply put, invasive species impoverish complex food webs, threaten biological diversity, cause extinctions, and reduce ecological resilience. Indeed, at this point, several questions remain to be answered, although in one radio interview Minister Matthew Samuda described the restocking process as "the beginning of the end" of the matter.

But that is not all. Fishermen remained nervous, but another report of dead fish in May was discounted by NEPA upon investigation. On 16 July, another fish kill was discovered in a different section of the Rio Cobre. Fishers reported that the water, further downstream and near an industrial complex, had "a black look." The latest media report quoted the National Environment and Planning Agency (NEPA), which confirmed that this was effluent from an unnamed, nearby factory, and that they had served an enforcement notice on the company on 18 July. NEPA says it may take further action. As the river struggles to recover, residents will have to wait until December this year before they may be able to start fishing again. Meanwhile, it is hoped that the major 2022 pollution event will be the last for this beautiful river and that it can begin regenerating.

Not Sure Where to Start?

Try to imagine a day in the life of a fish indigenous to the river Cobre.

What might have been the creature's daily schedule, from 5AM to 5PM in a time before the river was restocked with tilapia? What might be different about its schedule now?

By focusing on nothing more or less than the schedule of a fish's day, how might you articulate the changes that are voiced in the preceding article?

Text Fourteen

Fuel Price Increase Leads to Demonstrations and Deaths in Angola

> *This story by Global Voices Lusofonia (2023)*
> *originally appeared on Global Voices.*

On 1 June, the government of Angola, through the minister of state for economic coordination, Manuel Nunes Júnior, declared an increase in fuel prices in the country, following the government's announcement of the gradual withdrawal of gasoline subsidies. Thus, prices go from the previous 160 kwanzas to 300 kwanzas per litre (from USD 0.26 to USD 0.49), with the subsidy maintained for the agriculture and fishing sectors. Subsidies for other products such as diesel, cooking gas and lighting oil remain unchanged until the end of this year. According to the Minister, the tariffs for taxi drivers and motorcycle taxi drivers will be subsidized, and they will continue to pay 160 kwanzas per litre of gasoline, with the State covering the difference for an unspecified time. However, this subsidy does not cover all taxi drivers, so the day after the inception of the new prices, several cities in Angola woke up to demonstrations.

In reaction, there were reports of acts of violence carried out by the police against the demonstrators, mostly taxi drivers. One of the news reports even gave accounts of deaths caused by live bullets fired by the country's security forces. Mwene Vunongue, a social activist who has been following the situation in Angola tweeted about the situation that the "strike of taxi drivers and motorcycle taxi drivers rose in Lubango. Remember that yesterday there was a demonstration in Huambo, where the police killed five people. The rise in the price of gasoline and the non-assignment of a taxi driver's card is the central issue." There were other reports about the demonstrations, including from journalist and Human Rights Watch senior researcher, Zenaida Machado who said: "Angolan police fatally shoot against protest over fuel prices. Government should properly investigate and prosecute the deaths, with a view to introducing measures to instil respect for human rights in the security forces." Human rights activist, Luaty Beirão, displayed a poster that accused the country's ruling party, MPLA, of being the main driver of the indignation felt in the country. Other citizens denounced the use of live bullets, which is a recurring practice of the Angolan police during demonstrations. "It has a name: State Terrorism," one such individual wrote. "Just the fact that they advance, ostensibly, with the gun in hand and firing, without backfiring, is already something that goes beyond the red lines of any police force. The big problem is when these 'terrorists' are also caught in an alley."

On 17 June, Angolans protested again, and just as before, the police used force and violence to prevent the march from continuing. "Without any reason, the police decided to repress a demonstration that was taking place without any kind of shock or incident," the Civic Movement posted. "The rational person wonders why, but this goes beyond the logic of the democratic mind." The Angolan police admitted having used force against demonstrators in the provinces of Luanda and Benguela which they sought to justify by saying this was due to non-compliance with the routes established by the authorities. However, organizers denied these allegations and accused the police of shooting at unarmed people.

Not Sure Where to Start?

Write about an ordinary action for one of the police personnel in the article above and go into detail about every single aspect involved in their execution of it. For instance, write about the steps that a police officer must follow to clean and load their guns before they are deployed to stop a protest. As each step of the officer's ritualistic routine begins, consider what they might hear from beyond the windows and doors of the space they are in. With nothing but ambient sounds of ongoing protests, focus on every miniscule step that is involved in this individual's actions.

Text Fifteen

The Healing Love between Indigenous Women

> *This story by Muy Waso (2023) originally*
> *appeared on Global Voices.*

Love is in the details, and no one can convince me otherwise. That is why I am fascinated by art, because it is full of details that reflect the artist's total and boundless dedication. If we talk about plastic arts, those details can be in the minimal point of light inside the pupil of an eye that transforms it into an observing subject, or in the delicate way in which yellow paint can become the mid-afternoon sun. I have spent years of my life looking for these signs that reveal love, and without being arrogant, I can consider myself an expert in finding them. I not only see them, but also feel them. That's why the first time I saw Castro and CC together I recognized that love that comes from the details, and because of that magic, I was compelled to ask them for an interview to write the story that I share with you below.

I was in Phoenix, Arizona, in the US when I met them. They live there and that's where they carry out their resistance. I met them at Cahokia, a venture led by Native American women, which works to generate sustainable economies through the development of artistic projects that promote creativity, the recovery of ancestral memory and the strengthening of Indigenous entrepreneurship. Castro is Stephanie Guillermina's last name and nickname; she is 32 years old, born in Queens, New York. Her parents are from Colombia and Chile, and she is of Muisca and Mapuche descent. She identifies as Queer, and is a multidisciplinary artist, event planner, and doula. Carrie Sage Curley, better known as CC, born on the sacred lands of San Carlos Apache in Arizona 34 years ago, is a lesbian, multidisciplinary artist, community organizer, and cultural keeper. In 2020, the two met during devotions at the Apache Stronghold ceremonial centre at Oak Flat, a mountain sacred to the Apache. In 2022, after participating in an event, Women of the Desert, in Phoenix, they felt their paths were not two, but one, and they have been walking hand-in-hand ever since in the same direction. That direction is everything. They do not have a relationship, they have a healing purpose: to make Indigenous women visible and recover their wisdom through art. Recovering their image taken away by centuries of colonization is not a minor struggle, and that is one of their goals—to build their image away from the visual clichés imposed by the dominant white ideologies, and they do it by painting one mural at a time. Their artwork can be found in the streets of Phoenix, in galleries, in social spaces, and in private collections, portraying strong, free, and autonomous Indigenous women, with their lights and shadows.

In this regard, Castro says that she hopes "to capture an authentic representation of my ancestors through the lens of the spirits that guide me and my brush," "to provoke a connection to the Andes for those who have been displaced through migration," and "that my relatives and those who experience my art will feel the power and light that travelled through me. And that they see the beauty and deeper meaning of intergenerational wisdom and love." For CC, her art is a connection to herself and to her roots through culture. It is interrogating her existence. She says that she uses her art as a weapon "for the people." She expresses her love for painting "my people, especially the women. It is an honour to be Apache. Whoever comes across my work I want them to feel loved by their self, and proud." There is an ancestral voice that guides them and connects the past and the present to build a future, and those voices are materialized in art pieces. As CC explains: "We are our great-grandmothers, grandmothers, mothers. The clan is passed down from generation to generation. Our connection to the land is through our clan. I paint the strong women of the past and present." CC shares that her "mother is a local seamstress who continues to keep the spirit of dress alive. I photograph her work with my family and the women of the community, and that is why I am like this, I find my strength in my culture and the land." The story that both are building is deeply inspiring, for it is the story of liberation. The liberation of our bodies and our image. As Castro says, "I feel that colonization has robbed us of our sensuality and connection to our divine sexual power and energy. I work diligently to regain this sensual awareness and connection to my body and my sexual power." Castro believes that the "freer we are as individuals, the freer we are as a people. Returning to our ways in which we followed spirit and nature. Because our sexuality is divine nature—as plants and trees pollinate, so do we."

The sexual revolution is a pending issue in Latin America, and in Indigenous communities even more so; however, this story of transformation and light shows us that another reality is possible, where traditions, spirituality, and creativity are not at odds with sexual diversity, but rather complement each other and become one. In this regard, CC shares the following reflection for all those people who have an internal debate between their sexuality and their traditions. "You should know that there is nothing wrong with you," CC wants them to know. "Our creator gave you the spirit you carry. I know it can be scary to think what others say when they think of you but show them kindness and love because that is who you are. You need prayers, the earth, and people to be supported healthily."

I thank them for the moments I was able to enjoy their company and I thank them for allowing me to tell their story. I feel it is a duty to share the life of these powerful souls, so that the force that brought them together can be amplified, and their experience can inspire others to live a freer life, far from the shackles of puritanical glances that condemn the healing love between Indigenous women. As I finish writing this text, and my memory returns to the first day I met them. Castro looked at CC and smiled at her, and a whole universe opened up in the room. Planets, languages, silences, and ecosystems lived there that no one else could understand but them. And so, I reassert my stance: love is in the smallest details.

Not Sure Where to Start?

Imagine that Castro and CC asked you—wherever you are, whoever you are—to organize a wedding ceremony for them; a ritual or celebration that they asked you to design for them based on *your* customs. Write about the event you would organize for them and how you would adapt something that is familiar to you, for people who are not.

Works Cited

Global Voices Lusofonia. (2023). *Fuel price increase leads to demonstrations and deaths in Angola.* [Online] Global Voices. Available at: https://globalvoices.org/2023/07/17/fuel-price-increase-leads-to-demonstrations-and-deaths-in-angola/ [Accessed 28 Aug. 2023].

Lewis, E. (2023). *Fish are poured into Jamaica's Rio Cobre after pollution incidents, but is this the end of the matter?* [Online] Global Voices. Available at: https://globalvoices.org/2023/07/20/fish-are-poured-into-jamaicas-rio-cobre-after-pollution-incidents-but-is-this-the-end-of-the-matter/ [Accessed 28 Aug. 2023].

Waso, M. (2023). *The healing love between Indigenous women.* [Online] Global Voices. Available at: https://globalvoices.org/2023/06/30/the-healing-love-between-indigenous-women/ [Accessed 28 Aug. 2023].

Part Six

Explore Choices

As you create written responses to the news articles in this section, consider what kinds of invitations might be extended to a reader to enable them to make choices about their degrees of engagement and in so doing, craft avenues for self-directed learning and reflection.

One way to approach this integration of choice is considering a sensorial dimension that is traditionally not dominant in the aesthetic experience in question. For instance, reading tends to prioritize one dominant sensory focus: the visual, the tactile (Braille), or the auditory (audio books). What are ways to expand this understanding and consideration of what other kinds of reading experiences might be crafted so that the reader is asked to engage with more than one sensory stimulus?

Guided by the understanding that connecting with others' lives might often need multiple points of access for someone who doesn't have that experience, this strategy might resonate with something a teacher might employ in designing a lesson plan: the more modes through which an activity is engaged with, the higher the likelihood of the learning "sticking" for a larger number of students in the room.

How can we craft invitations that always allow the reader choice, without damaging what the story is able to communicate, even if that invitation is not accepted? How do we design invitations that are challenging, but that also exhibit care for the person who might (not) choose to engage with them?

DOI: 10.4324/9781032688749-9

How do we craft invitations that approach the central questions sensitively, ethically, and which don't fall into problematic modes that "gamify" someone else's reality?

Are there specific kinds of events or experiences—or degrees of "insider-ness" and "outsider-ness" with regard to the author's lived experience—that make the use of invitations to readers more or less ethically murky?

Text Sixteen

About 47,000 Russian Soldiers Died during the Full-scale Russian Invasion of Ukraine

This story by Daria Dergacheva (2023)
originally appeared on Global Voices.

According to a collaborative investigation conducted by Meduza, Mediazona, and statistician Dmitry Kobak from Tubingen University, the true number of Russian soldiers killed in the invasion of Ukraine is approximately 47,000. This estimate is based on an analysis of published obituaries, mortality data from the Federal State Statistics Service, and extensive records from the National Probate Registry. By examining these sources, the researchers estimated that between 40,000 and 55,000 Russian men under the age of 50 died in combat in Ukraine by 27 May 2023. When factoring in seriously wounded soldiers who did not return to military service, the total casualty count for Russia rises to at least 125,000 soldiers. The significance of these numbers becomes apparent when comparing them to previous conflicts. In just 15 months of fighting in Ukraine, three times more Russian soldiers have died than Soviet troops did over ten years in Afghanistan. Additionally, the death toll in Ukraine is nine times higher than the casualties in the first Russian–Chechen War from 1994 to 1996. These figures highlight not only the high number of lives lost in Vladimir Putin's aggressive war but also the authorities' deliberate efforts to conceal the true costs of the invasion from the Russian public.

The Russian government has classified information about casualties, and revealing the deaths of Russian soldiers in Ukraine on social media can lead to prosecution by Russian police. The Defence Ministry has not provided updated casualty figures since September 2022, up to which point they claimed that only 5,937 Russian soldiers had been killed in the "special military operation." However, given the nature of war, it is unlikely that the Russian military's own casualty figures can be accepted as accurate, as each side tends to exaggerate the enemy's losses while downplaying their own. The most reliable public information about Russia's losses in the war comes from a database created by independent monitors working with journalists at Mediazona and the BBC. This database tracks combat deaths mentioned in local news outlets and on social media. As of now, the database shows nearly 27,000 Russian soldiers killed in Ukraine. However, this number represents only a fraction of the total casualties, as many deaths go unreported due to various reasons such as fear of prosecution, the involvement of foreign nationals fighting in the Russian military, and the release of prison inmates to fight in Ukraine.

To provide a more accurate estimate, the investigative journalists from Meduza and Mediazona obtained access to a restricted but non-classified database of inheritance cases. By comparing trends in this database with publicly available demographics and previous reporting on obituaries, they were able to estimate the total number of Russian soldiers killed in Ukraine as of late May 2023 to be approximately 47,000. The database covers over 11 million individual cases since 2014, and although it is not comprehensive, the large sample size makes the data representative and reliable for this analysis.

Not Sure Where to Start?

As the reader reads the names of the 47,000 soldiers who have died—names that you locate via archival research—invite them to place a grain of rice on a surface beside them, a beat between reading about each lost life and a tactile moment of witness and recognition.

Text Seventeen

*Aboriginal Australian Journalist Stan Grant Steps
down from Post after Enduring Racial Abuse*

> *This story by Mong Palatino (2023) originally
> appeared on Global Voices.*

Veteran Indigenous journalist Stan Grant took a break from his role as program host and columnist for the Australian Broadcasting Corporation (ABC) after he was targeted by racist attacks during the broadcaster's coverage of the coronation of the United Kingdom's King Charles III.

Grant, who belongs to the Wiradjuri Aboriginal people, has been a journalist for over three decades. He was the host for ABC's current affairs program Q+A and a regular columnist for ABC News online. Grant wrote on 19 May about the racist vitriol against him and his family following his guesting on a TV panel about the colonial legacy of the British monarchy and particularly its impact on Australia's aboriginal population. Some conservatives frowned on the timing of the show which was aired hours before the coronation of King Charles.

Grant explained his reason for taking leave by saying: "I am writing this because no one at ABC—whose producers invited me onto their coronation coverage as a guest—has uttered one word of public support. Not one ABC executive has publicly refuted the lies written or spoken about me. I don't hold any individual responsible; this is an institutional failure." He also reflected on how the "media has turned public discussion into an amusement park" and described social media as a "grotesque burlesque" where "lives are reduced to mockery and ridicule." He added, "I take time out because we have shown again that our history—our hard truth—is too big, too fragile, too precious for the media. The media sees only battle lines, not bridges. It sees only politics. I want no part of it. I want to find a place of grace far from the stench of the media. I want to go where I am not reminded of the social media sewer." During the final episode of his show, he addressed his fellow Wiradjuri people: "To my people—I have always wanted to represent you with pride. I know I might disappoint you sometimes, but in my own little way, I've just wanted to make us seen. And I'm sorry that I can't do that for a little while."

ABC news director Justin Stevens said he regretted not having come to Grant's defence before and released a statement accusing other media outlets of fuelling the hatred against Grant. "The responsibility for the coverage lies with ABC News management, not with Stan Grant," the release stated. "Yet it is he who has borne the brunt of a tirade of criticism, particularly in the usual sections of the media that target the ABC." Stevens acknowledges that reporting "on his contribution to the panel discussion has been unfair, inaccurate and irresponsible. It has contributed to fuelling horrendous personal and racial abuse." During an interview with *The Guardian*, Stevens accused Rupert Murdoch's News Corp of leading the pile-on against Grant. But News Corp Australasia chief executive Michael Miller said the charge was "misleading" and "unsubstantiated" and urged ABC "to stop passing the buck and blaming others for its own internal problems." On 22 May, staff members of ABC in several cities gathered outside their offices to express solidarity with Grant and to protest racism. The Twitter/X hashtag #istandwithstan shows the support received by Grant on social media. ABC managing director David Anderson has formally apologized to Grant. Furthermore, the Media, Entertainment & Arts Alliance, the union of Australian media workers, noted that the issue should lead to more conversations and actions about protecting journalists from abuse: "We must take this terrible moment to properly grasp what we are facing and to ensure that the workers who tell our stories can continue to perform their vital public service free from abuse and danger."

Not Sure Where to Start?

Invite the reader to imagine themselves as a reporter for *their* community, whatever that might be. Then, ask them to imagine what they would say if they were in Stan Grant's position and tasked with providing a positive commentary about a person, group, or institution that has caused damage to their community. How would you craft this invitation?

How would you create enough support for a reader who has no experience with such interactive invitations, while also including enough novelty for readers who might crave this type of engagement?

Text Eighteen

In Turkey, Even University Graduations Are Political

> *This story by Arzu Geybullayeva (2023)*
> *originally appeared on Global Voices.*

Ankara's qualms with the country's education system have been ongoing since the ruling Justice and Development Party (AKP) came to power in 2002. Interventions into the education landscape began subtly—if not inclusively—at first, but over the years, they were replaced with efforts to reform the curriculum along more religious lines and deeper control mechanisms. These days, independent experts say Turkey's education system is in decline. But it is not just the curriculum or the structure that the state is intervening in. In recent years, even graduation ceremonies have been heavily scrutinized, at times, getting cancelled altogether despite students' and academics' demands to reverse the decision.

Protests and Creative Banners

In an email sent to the students of Bogazici University on 31 May ahead of their graduation ceremonies, the students were informed that the school's management had decided there wouldn't be a collective graduation ceremony as had been a tradition at the end of each academic year. Instead, each department would hold separate ceremonies in separate locations on campus. This is the second year they implemented dispersed graduation ceremonies, according to reporting by *Diken* newspaper. The change was implemented purportedly to stave off any potential student protest or organizing.

Last year, despite the ban, students organized their own collective graduation ceremonies, prompting university administrators to cancel all their graduate IDs that grant them access to the school, effectively blocking their access to the campus. The move was not surprising, given that since 2021, the university students and its academic staff have been protesting the appointment of a new rector, who was handpicked by President Recep Tayyip Erdoğan. While the controversial government-appointed rector, Melih Bulu, has since been removed, the protests continue at the prestigious school as another appointee replaced him. The school has an extensive internal election process, so the two external appointments were viewed as a "breach of academic freedom as it bypassed rectorate elections and was the first time a person from outside the university had been placed in the rectoral seat since the coup of 12 September 1980," reported Gazete Duvar at the time.

An attempt to also cancel the collective graduation ceremony at the Middle East Technical University (METU) was reversed last minute following protests from students. According to reports, the university's administration decided to move ahead with holding a collective ceremony at the campus stadium. However, the school warned attendees that all banners would be closely scrutinized. Several graduation ceremonies were also cancelled at the university in recent years on the grounds of a security threat out of concern that students might criticize the state through banners or protests. In 2019, at least five METU students were arrested ahead of the graduation ceremony out of fear of provocation. Last year, when the university administration said the collective graduation ceremony was cancelled, a statement signed by METU Alumni Association called on the rectorate to reverse the decision. When the rectorate did not budge, faculty members and students organized the ceremony themselves. There was a heavy police presence, and students were only allowed to invite immediate family members.

Bogazici, METU, and other progressive, independent universities are known for their graduation ceremonies, where new graduates carry banners with political, cultural, and social messages. Banners held by students during this year's graduation at METU focused on the country's failing economy, women's rights, and living conditions—mostly addressed with humour. A message from the graduates of the Mathematics Department read, "Our math skills and knowledge were insufficient to calculate the amount of money collected for the earthquake survivors which then vanished." Or the banner carried by the graduates of the Physics Department that read, "The way to read Einstein's $E = mc^2$ formula within our country's context. e (inflation—in Turkish "enflasyon") = m (current situation—in Turkish "mevcut sistem") c (ignorance—in Turkish "cehalet") ^{2}." Another banner read, "Turkey's new century is going to be tremendous." The word "tremendous" in Turkish translates as "muazzam" and the students highlighted the last three letters "zam" which means "price hike" or "raise," in Turkish (a tongue-in-cheek reference to a series of price hikes that have been implemented in the country because of financial difficulties.) Another popular act of solidarity was sent to the country's LGBTQ+ community with students unfolding a large rainbow flag.

In some instances, students decided to raise their concerns individually, like Melisa Caymaz, who unfurled a rainbow flag during her graduation ceremony in the province of Usak. Caymaz faced death threats and public shaming while the university said it has launched formal proceedings against the student. The anti-LGBTQ+ ire extends not only to universities. When a primary school in Istanbul set up a rainbow-decorated wall for its graduation ceremony, the school's director and one teacher were fired from their jobs after the former mayor of Ankara, İbrahim Melih Gökçek raised the issue on Twitter/X: "If this woman is a teacher, she must immediately be fired. Those who push our children towards homosexuality, are murderers of our children."

For the former mayor, anything that includes rainbow colours is LGBTQ+ propaganda. In another tweet, he targeted a hospital in the province of Kocaeli for having its exterior hospital panels painted in bright colours. More generally, under the AKP rule, the emphasis on family values and the portrayal of LGBTQ+ people as a threat to these values has been part of a narrative weaponized by local politicians, including President Erdoğan. The ruling party has long viewed the community as a "virus" and "poison."

Raising Pious Generations

The country's independent education experts have been raising concerns about the decay of the education system for over a decade. They argued that the existing system was being remodelled in line with the ruling government's bid to raise "pious generations" and forge a "New Turkey." These efforts date back to 2012 when under the leadership of the then-Prime Minister Erdoğan, Turkey replaced the old system where compulsory education consisted of five years of primary and three years of secondary school (5+3) with four-year phases for primary, secondary, and high school (4+4+4) without allowing any consultation or debate. Although progressive at first look—raising compulsory education to an additional four years—the change subjected children to religious education at an earlier age. It allowed the secondary education tier to be replaced by imam-hatip (vocational schools to educate imams and preachers) schools, which offered Islamic education to students at high-school level only. Other changes introduced by the state—such as centralized admission exams to all secondary and high schools in 2014—"transformed the religious schools from a selective option to a central institution in the education system," wrote columnist Orhan Kemal Cengiz, who explained that if a student failed to get a certain amount of points to secure entry to a public school, they would have no other choice but to enrol at an imam-hatip school. According to a 2018 Reuters investigation, spending on imam-hatip schools doubled by 2018, and the number of enrolled pupils rose fivefold. Since then, scores of new imam-hatip schools have opened.

In 2016, the state also introduced a new measure that required all candidate teachers to pass an Oral Exam Evaluation. The exam was criticized by several education syndicates at the time for its opaque structure and irrelevance. In their evaluation, syndicates raised concerns that while Oral Exam Evaluation was a practice also used in other countries, in Turkey it was the primary method that determined whether a potential candidate could become a teacher. The new measures came a month after the failed military coup of 2016. Following the coup, over 100,000 people were removed or suspended from their jobs, among them more than 30,000 teachers, 5,000 academics, deans, and others. Many viewed the purges within universities as the state's attempt to deal with dissenters, especially at the universities the state previously had no control over. In 2016, Erdoğan secured the right to appoint university rectors who were previously elected by each school's academic body. In 2017, the theory of evolution was removed from the teaching curriculum at Turkish schools despite criticism. In July 2023, Turkish Education Minister Yusuf Tekin suggested the establishment of all-girls schools—a statement he has since backtracked on due to public outcry. What the state fails to see, however, is the long-term impact of such severe control mechanisms. Owing to the purges following the failed coup attempt, as well as growing polarization, many people have either left or are considering leaving. Speaking to BNE Intellnews, Bekir Agirdir, director of the Konda research consultancy, notes that although the brain drain is not new, the reasons for leaving have become more political.

Not Sure Where to Start?

Ask the reader to go to a Turkish restaurant in their city—one that is run by people from that country—and invite them to engage with *one* dish on the menu. Invite them to learn more about the history of that dish by engaging with the person making or serving their food and, if the opportunity presents itself, to invite the sharer of the food to describe any national or social or cultural significance of that menu item.

In turn, in your written response to Turkey's educational circumstances, share your own attempt to carry out the task that you are giving to the reader.

What insights did your in-person interaction allow you to gain about the themes put forward in the preceding article? And if the conversation did not yield anything related to the themes of the article, use your real-world interaction as a starting point for an imagined one. What are the questions you might ask if you were to meet the Turkish restaurant owner again?

Use the impetus of writing about someone else's lived experience to engage with people from that background or heritage in your geographical radius, always making sure to carefully consider which types of engagement might be more or less ethically murky than others.

The least problematic starting points, in my experience—if there is no one from that place in your personal networks—is to engage with those who have chosen to be in people-centric professions that draw focus to their specific cultures: restaurants are great starting points, as are artistic or cultural ensembles.

Works Cited

Dergacheva, D. (2023). *About 47,000 Russian soldiers died during the full-scale Russian invasion of Ukraine.* [Online] Global Voices. Available at: https://globalvoices.org/2023/07/11/about-47000-russian-soldiers-died-during-the-full-scale-russian-invasion-of-ukraine/ [Accessed 28 Aug. 2023].

Geybullayeva, A. (2023). *In Turkey, even university graduations are political*. [Online] Global Voices. Available at: https://globalvoices.org/2023/08/01/in-turkey-even-university-graduations-are-political/ [Accessed 28 Aug. 2023].

Palatino, M. (2023). *Aboriginal Australian journalist Stan Grant steps down from post after enduring racial abuse*. [Online] Global Voices. Available at: https://globalvoices.org/2023/05/28/aboriginal-australian-journalist-stan-grant-steps-down-from-post-after-enduring-racial-abuse/ [Accessed 28 Aug. 2023].

Part Seven

Explore Unresolved Endings

Many writers, when introduced to the art of storytelling, are taught to end with conflict resolution. And while this approach might be of use in a range of storylines and types, *not* having a resolution could present an ethical strategy when outsiders are writing about experiences they have not lived. So, whatever way you choose to create a written response to the news articles in this section, focus on ways you might showcase an *absence* of resolution.

Might an intentional abandonment of resolution allow a more ethical engagement wherein an outsider does not attempt to resolve a reality that they have no lived experience of?

What kinds of unfinished endings capture complexity without creating absolute helplessness and hopelessness in its readers?

Are there specific kinds of events or incidences—or degrees of "insider-ness" and "outsider-ness" with regard to the author's lived experience—that might make the use of unresolved or unfinished endings more or less ethically murky?

Text Nineteen

"Indigenous Languages Are Asleep, Not Extinct,"
Says Kokama linguistics Researcher

This story by Amazônia Real (2023) originally
appeared on Global Voices.

DOI: 10.4324/9781032688749-10

The brutality against Indigenous people in Brazil has promoted not only the loss of their territories but also extinguished many original languages. There were over 1,000 native languages when the European invaders landed in the country in 1500. Today there are just more than 200, according to the Brazilian Institute of Geography and Statistics (IBGE). With the review following data from the 2022 Census, this number could increase. In some cases, there are barely any speakers, with only one or two people keeping the language alive. But there are many ways to recover, revitalize and rescue an original people's language, even those considered to be extinct. Through rituals and contacts with ancestors, the so-called spirit-languages can be "resurrected."

With this idea in mind, professor and researcher Altaci Rubim took an important part in the Indigenous Languages International Decade, a global mobilization instituted by the United Nations that started in 2022 and will go on until 2032.

Altaci is the Latin America and Caribbean representative at UNESCO's working group for this campaign. According to UNESCO, there are over 7,000 spoken languages on the planet. Of those, over 6,000 are Indigenous, but 3,000 are at risk of disappearing. Among the reasons that could lead a language to extinction are factors such as speakers dying, colonizers or missionaries forbidding it being spoken, territorial destruction, racism, and discrimination. In 2022, the death of a Tanaru Indigenous man, known as "the Indigenous in a hole," was the end of a linguistic treasure that lived only with him.

Altaci is from the Kokama people in the Amazonas state. She is a researcher, activist and has just taken up a position in the Department of Indigenous Languages and Memory in the recently created Indigenous People's Ministry. Her name in their language is Tataiya Kokama. In Manaus, Amazonas' capital, where she lived through a significant part of her working life, Altaci developed the revitalization of her people's language in communities within urban contexts. She describes herself as a linguist "by profession and by heart," who dialogues with anthropology and other sciences. In an interview with Amazônia Real, she speaks of the efforts to preserve languages at risk.

Amazônia Real: What is the Indigenous Languages International Decade?

It came up in 2019, in Bolivia, during a fight to strengthen Indigenous languages. In this movement, the International Year of Indigenous Languages was created. UNESCO then opened a call to institutions to dialogue with Indigenous people, and organizations to prepare an action plan with the people in the seven regions of the planet.

Amazônia Real: Why was it necessary to create a decade for the Indigenous languages?

First, because the planet is risking extinction. UNESCO knows that Indigenous languages also keep the knowledge of those who preserve the forests, fighting problems brought by fires, by the pollution in the rivers. The climate issues are minimized from the traditional knowledges that are contained in Indigenous languages. Evidently there are many actions to avoid the disappearance of the planet, but Indigenous languages represent one of the possibilities to fight this. So, leaders, rulers are being called to create politics of appreciation, maintenance, retaking and strengthening of the Indigenous languages.

Amazônia Real: How did Indigenous languages disappear and why do they need to be brought back?

In Latin America and the Caribbean, there are around 58.2 million Indigenous people, speaking around 550 original languages. In Brazil, at the beginning of the colonization process there were over 1,000 languages. It was a set of actions: the church, the state's own dominance politics. Everything adds up to removing Indigenous people from their lands. All those policies were conducted to end the lives of original people. But the colonizers knew that one day we would wake up, know who we are, the value of our languages. That is why they needed to end our memory and resistance. The first tool used was the language, through silencing. There were politics of extermination, diseases, slavery, massacres. Another thing was to diminish the land demarcation until there was no one left.

Amazônia Real: What will be done during this decade? What actions are being planned?

We were called with other people to elaborate a plan of world action to the decade. From that plan on, we will start to organize. I applied through the Kokama Indigenous Association from Manaus. We are building self-sufficiency in Brazil, so we can walk with our own legs. To make this movement continue beyond the decade.

Amazônia Real: What will be done to enhance languages at risk?

Working with languages is conflicting. But if we do not ally in this moment, we may not have the opportunity to strengthen languages that are "weak." There are some people who want to retake it but lack public policies to do so. Before, researchers who had their niches of research to a determined language did not open space to anyone else, not even to the own people [those who were being topic of research].

Amazônia Real: What did you find extraordinary so far in the initial mapping of Indigenous languages in Brazil?

The Indigenous sign language called my attention, something that has always existed among Indigenous people, how they communicate. Nowadays we have the Brazilian Sign Language (Libras) even disrespecting what the own people have. It doesn't mean you shouldn't learn it [the non-Indigenous sign language], but that the signs used by the Indigenous people in their communities shouldn't be undermined. Some researchers even work with the subject of Indigenous Portuguese. It's an important subject for us, but we didn't find a way of having Indigenous people speaking out about it, which is the demand of speaking only the official Portuguese language to the detriment of the Portuguese with Indigenous influence, in memory.

Amazônia Real: What is Indigenous Portuguese?

An example is the Portuguese spoken by the Tikuna people (people from the region of the High Solimões river), but with their influence, the Portuguese spoken by the Kokama. There are 370 ways of speaking Portuguese, because every people will do it according to their language. Why are we bringing up this discussion? Because all policies of teacher training need to take into consideration those who speak an Indigenous language and those who have Portuguese as a second language. This is another way of thinking about training.

Amazônia Real: You've commented about a concept called "water truce." What is it and how does it relate to Indigenous Languages?

We know that before these discussions, before we had graduated Indigenous people, institutions who had control over Indigenous people were the ones doing research. Many will give it back to their people, other wouldn't. What has been recorded is a treasure for us. Slowly we can start to socialize it. Putting these questions is discussion, so the researchers can go to other people as well. We want our language because it's our life. Knowledge is the spirit of the people. We are not criminalizing [the researchers], because it was the thought of that time. But today we are talking and placing the "water truce."

It means we need to stop fighting among ourselves, break the wall and say that we all need to drink some water, we all need the Indigenous languages. It's a metaphor for the current times.

Amazônia Real: How does one analyse Indigenous languages today?

The Indigenous languages were always categorized by non-Indigenous linguists. They got the Eurocentric European organization, which categorizes Neo-latin languages, for example, to categorize Indigenous ones too. Which is another perspective. Today, we the Indigenous people heading this discussion, have another way of seeing it. According to the classification of Aryon Rodrigues [a Brazilian linguist, who died in 2014], there are 180 languages nowadays in Brazil. It used to be 1,100 back at the colonizer arrival.

Amazônia Real: What is the difference between the conception of languages in the light of classical thinkers, such as Saussure [Swiss linguist], and Indigenous connoisseurs and researchers?

If you go with Saussure, we'll have language as a system. In Noam Chomsky's conception, the conception of language is given in the universal grammar. It's another way of thinking. In our conception of language, we also have the spirit-language. Our spirits only speak in each people's own language. Knowing that there is a spirit-language, then this conception is that it doesn't die, it can't be considered extinct.

Amazônia Real: Where is the spirit-language present?

They are retaken in dreams, by the spirit. Many people have it in memory or kept in another place, like a museum. Those who don't have it, are woken up in these rituals.

Amazônia Real: Which are the other categories of languages that go by this process of rescue?

We have languages being revitalized, languages asleep and languages in maintenance. Languages in revitalization are not spoken in daily life, but it has elder speakers. There is a whole base to be retaken. Revitalization is to give strength to the dynamics of existence, which happens from singing, from rituals. One of the languages being revitalized is the Patxohã, from the Pataxó people, in the state of Bahia. They collectively decided to speak the language. But the lexicon they had was short. There were only two people who remembered. So, they moved to rituals. From their dreams and rituals, they created new lexicons. The language was updated. Today the language is a full process of revitalization. Languages in maintenance, for example, include the Tikuna's. There are communities that don't speak anymore; therefore, it needs a policy for maintenance. There are cases of communities where is weakening.

Amazônia Real: How do you rescue a language that, in a standard understanding, was considered extinct?

Some of the most important ones are the languages that are asleep, but they were not extinct. For example, the Manaós' language. It can be awakened in rituals. From the moment that someone claims the identity, they can want their language back. It can get in touch with the spirits. This is our perspective of debate for the decade.

Amazônia Real: How can we understand the spirit-languages without turning it into an exotic piece under the lights of non-Indigenous people?

When one speaks about spirit it's assumed that they are talking about religiosity. But we are talking about it in the conception of the original people. The spirit has a meaning, but according to the spirituality of each people.

Amazônia Real: In the city of Manaus, the population of the Kokama people is strong and numerous. How is the work with the Kokama group that lives in the capital of Amazonas state?

I have kept this fight since 2000. But throughout this path, we had to deconstruct ourselves along the process. To take out the colonizer spirit that we learned. People couldn't believe that I spoke my language. They didn't hear me speaking. So, it's necessary to demystify it. To understand that linguistic processes are important to say: "I speak Kokama, I teach Kokama." While I didn't understand that, while I didn't go through a training that allowed that, I continued as many others, without being able to understand and to speak it. With the Kokama group we held training workshops.

Amazônia Real: How is the language of your people, the Kokama?

We, the Kokama, held an assembly and decided to keep the official language spoken in Peru [the kukama language turned official in the country in 2015]. Among our Kokama group, the one which I belong to, we keep this deal. It's this common language that we speak.

Not Sure Where to Start?

End your story with something unexpected. For instance, write about the battle between the languages described in the article above as if it were a tug of war. And just when it seems like one side—one army—might have a slightly upper hand, as if they might become the victor in this fight, introduce a stimulus that comes as a surprise to *both* linguistic armies.
An explosion.
An unexpected antagonist.
An earthquake.
End your story there.

Text Twenty

Camacho-Quinn's Historic Olympic Win Sparks
Discussion on Puerto Rican Identity

> *This story by Ángel Carrión (2021)*
> *originally appeared on Global Voices.*

On the night of 1 August, Puerto Ricans everywhere celebrated with rapturous joy Jasmine Camacho-Quinn's gold medal win for the women's 100-metre hurdles at the Olympics in Tokyo. With Puerto Rico having to endure so much negative news about its fiscal woes, gender-based violence, and deteriorating public services and infrastructure, all while surviving the COVID-19 pandemic, Camacho-Quinn's historic gold medal brings a much welcome bit of good news.

Camacho-Quinn is only the second Puerto Rican ever to win a gold medal for the Caribbean island. Tennis player Mónica Puig was the first when she won five years ago in Rio de Janeiro. But her accomplishments don't stop there. In the semi-finals, she obtained an Olympic record-setting time of 12.26 seconds, breaking the previous record of 12.35 seconds held by Australian Sally Peterson. This also makes Camacho-Quinn the first Puerto Rican to set an Olympic record. Her story is one of perseverance. In the semi-finals during her first Olympics in 2016, her leg clipped the top of the eighth hurdle (of a total of ten), impeding her from regaining her form before the ninth and causing her to fall.

Lawyer and human rights activist Eva Prados pointed out some important facts about this important event. "Did you know that our first and only Olympic gold medals have been won by two WOMEN under the administration of the first WOMAN [Sara Rosario] that presides the [Puerto Rico] Olympic Committee?" Prados asks her readers.

Camacho-Quinn is a Puerto Rican from the diaspora and lives in the United States. Even though Puerto Rico is not an independent country, but a US territory, the IOC has recognized Puerto Rico as its own team competing separately from the US Olympic team since 1948; thus, athletes can choose which country to represent. Camacho-Quinn decided to represent her mother's homeland of Puerto Rico. Some Puerto Ricans questioned whether she could be considered Puerto Rican, since she was born and raised in the US, while others fiercely defended her for choosing to represent Puerto Rica, such as educator and activist, Xiomara Torres Rivera, who wrote the following on Todas, an online magazine dedicated to journalism from a feminist perspective. "Quite a few people have taken the time to say that Jasmine isn't Puerto Rican because she doesn't even train here [in Puerto Rico]." Rivera says that to "this discussion we could add the calls to both the Puerto Rico Olympic Committee and the government to improve the conditions of the athletes that do train here and do not manage to bring medals, but that's a different issue." She explains how "sports have always been a way to declare our existence before the world. Of naming ourselves as something else and to insist on reaffirming that we are not US Americans, that we are Puerto Ricans."

Clinical psychologist and professor at Harvard Medical School, Jenny Zhen Duan, who identifies as Puerto Rican and Chinese, wrote that she could relate well to the criticisms launched at Camacho-Quinn. She uses the example from the last Olympics where "people wouldn't stop judging 'how Puerto Rican' Mónica Puig was if 'she couldn't speak Spanish well and wasn't raised on the island.'" Duan mentions "seeing the same discourse with Jasmine Camacho-Quinn. Don't you get tired of isolating others? I've lived it my whole life and it's exhausting." Adding to this discussion neuroscientist and professor at Yale University, Daniel Colón Ramos, gave his definition of what it means to be Puerto Rican, while making another equally important point about the lack of support for Puerto Rican athletes training in Puerto Rico. "There's a legitimate question to reflect on Camacho-Quinn's accomplishments when considering how many more athletes would become like her if the ones that train here [in Puerto Rico] would get the support they need," Ramos says. "Aside from that, to me, a Puerto Rican is someone who loves Puerto Rico and works hard for the homeland. Everything else just diminishes the merits of those who choose to represent our flag."

Journalist Alejandra Jover also pointed out one other important fact about Camacho-Quinn that hasn't received the attention it deserves in the conversation surrounding her Olympic victory: her ethnicity. In her Twitter/X thread, Jover explains why this is so important to celebrate. "Do you know why it's important?" Jover asks, "because there are many, TOO MANY black Puerto Rican girls and women who have been made to feel as if they're somehow less because of the colour of their skin, because of their natural hair, because of their features. Because of their blackness. And Jasmine now represents and gives a face to the struggle of defending Puerto Rico's African roots, that many reject." Perhaps the most eloquent comment about Camacho-Quinn came from Marisol LeBrón, professor of Feminist Studies at the University of California in Santa Cruz, who managed to capture in a tweet a very common Puerto Rican experience: "With Camacho-Quinn's gold medal, Puerto Rico joins the celebration in the Caribbean with Bermuda's and Jamaica's victories, made even more significant by the fact that they've all been accomplished by women."

Not Sure Where to Start?

End with a choice that needs to be made. For example, just as Camacho-Quinn wins the Olympics, maybe she receives—at the same time—phone calls both from the President of the United States and the Governor of Puerto Rico. Whose call will she choose to answer?

When an outsider is trying to understand experiences that we haven't lived, maybe we have no idea where endings begin or where beginnings end.

Text Twenty-One

New Zealand Government Apologizes for Dawn Raids
Targeting Pacific Communities in the 1970s

> *This story by Mong Palatino (2021) originally appeared*
> *on Global Voices.*

New Zealand Prime Minister, Jacinda Ardern, offered a "formal and unreserved apology" to the country's Pacific communities for dawn raids conducted by the police and immigration authorities in the 1970s. The raids lasted from March 1974 until 1976. During that time, New Zealand conducted hundreds of raids between 11pm and 3am to arrest and deport individuals who were "overstaying" in the country. Authorities were accused of discriminating against Pacific communities.

New Zealand encouraged Pacific nations to send workers after World War II, which helped expand the country's manufacturing sector. But during the recession of the early 1970s, there was an unemployment spike which was unfairly blamed on the influx of migrants from Pacific nations. This was followed by random inspections and interrogations targeting migrants from Pacific communities and their families.

During her apology, Arden described how community members "were hauled to the police station to appear in court the next day barefoot, in pyjamas, or in clothes loaned to them in the holding cells; others were wrongfully detained." Ardern made her apology during a town hall meeting in Auckland on 1 August 2021. "I stand before you as a symbol of the Crown that wronged you nearly 50 years ago," Ardern said. "Today, I stand on behalf of the New Zealand Government to offer a formal and unreserved apology to Pacific communities for the discriminatory implementation of the immigration laws of the 1970s that led to the events of the dawn raids." The Prime Minister went on to state that the "Government expresses its sorrow, remorse, and regret that the dawn raids and random police checks occurred and that these actions were ever considered appropriate." Minister for Pacific Peoples Aupito William Sio, who was born in Samoa, linked the dawn raids with racism. "The harm that was caused on a proud people was wrong. We now know that this was racism of the worst kind." Sio explained how "huge numbers of overstayers from Europe and America were basically left untouched. It was wrong then, it is wrong today, it will always be wrong—racism, discrimination, prejudice—whatever form it takes is wrong."

Tonga Princess Mele Siu'ilikutapu Kalaniuvalu Fotofili accepted Ardern's apology by saying "I am very grateful to your Government for making the right decision to apologise to right the extreme, inhumane, racist, and unjust treatment specifically against my community in the dawn raids era." The Princess assured the Prime Minister that "we have accepted the fact that some of our people at the time were on the wrong side of the law—yes. This should not have warranted the unleashing of police dogs on our people, the raids of our houses in the early hours of the morning, and many other extreme measures put in place at the time."

The enduring memory of this historic event, beyond the sight of the ritual ifoga covering of Ardern and the tears—from Tongan Princess to commoner pictured high in the town hall on the livestream—beyond the singing and moments of laughter, will be a few minutes of profound audio played at the beginning. In a silent town hall, a series of loud knocks on doors—knocks, bangs, thuds, dogs barking, faint sirens, people distressed, babies crying. These were the sounds of injustice.

Ardern announced several programs including over $3.1 million in scholarships and fellowships for Pacific youth, as well as additional resources to educate younger generations about the hurtful legacy of the dawn raids.

Not Sure Where to Start?

Craft multiple endings to your story.

Ending 1: what does Ardern's apology do—best-case scenario—for New Zealand?

Ending 2: what is the worst-case scenario?

Ending 3: what is another option?

Give your reader a sense of all possible outcomes because, especially as an outsider (and often, even as an insider), you have no way of knowing what comes next.

Works Cited

Amazônia Real. (2023). *'Indigenous languages are asleep, not extinct,'* *says Kokama linguistics researcher.* [Online] Global Voices. Available at: https://globalvoices.org/2023/07/26/indigenous-languages-are-asleep-not-extinct-says-kokama-linguistics-researcher/ [Accessed 28 Aug. 2023].

Carrión, Á. (2021). *Camacho-Quinn's historic Olympic win sparks discussion on Puerto Rican identity.* [Online] Global Voices. Available at: https://globalvoices.org/2021/08/06/camacho-quinns-historic-olympic-win-sparks-discussion-on-puerto-rican-identity/ [Accessed 28 Aug. 2023].

Palatino, M. (2021). *New Zealand government apologizes for dawn raids targeting Pacific communities in the 1970s.* [Online] Global Voices. Available at: https://globalvoices.org/2021/08/06/new-zealand-government-apologizes-for-dawn-raids-targeting-pacific-communities-in-the-1970s/ [Accessed 28 Aug. 2023].

Section Three

Experiment!

As you go through this section, use the QR code or the footnoted link to visit the online forum for this book and share thoughts or questions from your experiments.[1]

1 https://nanditadinesh.com/creative-writing-and-the-experiences-of-others

DOI: 10.4324/9781032688749-11

Experiments

Experiment #1

Apply one or more of the seven strategies we've examined and explored to write about a context that is *extremely familiar* to you; one that you consider yourself more of an insider to; something you have lived experience of.

Share your writing with others who share your "insider-ness" of that context and ask them what they would add (or remove).

Consider what their feedback reveals about the ways in which you tend to engage. You might consider filling out a table like this one:

What did I miss?	Why might I have missed it?	How might I catch similar misses in future?

DOI: 10.4324/9781032688749-12

Experiment #2

Apply one or more of the strategies we've examined and explored to write about a context that is *somewhat familiar* to you *and* that you know someone from.

Share your writing with the person you know, who is more of an insider to the context or experience than you are. Ask them to look at your description and (i) correct any misconceptions and (ii) fill in any blanks. Invite them to think through with you the ways in which you might have been more ethical, more sensitive, more accurate in your writing.

Compare your process of creating the work in Experiment #1 with that which you've created in Experiment #2. Use your collaborator's feedback to reinvestigate the gaps in your process. Pay special attention to aspects you might have over-simplified, exoticized, or problematically othered.

Use Experiment #2 and the opportunity of having someone from that context as a source of feedback to identify any additional blinders that you might have when it comes to imagining experiences that you are more of an outsider to.

You might consider filling out a table like this one:

What did I miss?	Why might I have missed it?	Why did the strategies I designed in Experiment #1 to catch misses not work in this case?	How can I refine my strategy to identify such gaps in the future?

Experiment #3

Apply one or more of the strategies we've examined and explored to write about a context that is *completely unfamiliar* to you *and* that you know no one from. Once you have a draft, use what you've discovered about your process in Experiment #2 to locate the gaps in your own writing. Critique yourself; you might consider filling out a table like this one *before* doing so:

Based on what I noticed about my process in Experiments #1 and #2, what do I want to make sure I check for?

Always, *always* when you are writing about contexts that are completely unfamiliar, attempt to locate collaborators who will give you honest feedback; collaborators who are insiders to the experience that you are writing about. This can take a variety of forms:

- Individuals in your network who might know insiders to the experience.

- Organizations in your local setting, where you can engage directly with insiders to the experience (always beginning with spaces where your presence is likely to be *least* intrusive, like restaurants or artistic/cultural groups—work that has embedded within it a dimension of engaging with others).
- Cold call insider-artists or insider-educators outside your local context and ask them if they would be willing to offer insight (again, begin with individuals whose work has embedded within it a dimension of engaging with others).

In all of the abovementioned cases, try to find multiple, differently positioned stakeholders and, when feedback is given, try to factor in the host-guest/insider-outsider dynamics that might be at play. How can you create the conditions for honest feedback about the limitations to your imagination? How can you ensure that you are not being told what you want to hear?

Conclusion—One Last Thing

Despite your best efforts to integrate the strategies outlined here, or your past, present, or future endeavours to devise new ones, or your earnest attempts to write about experiences that you are an outsider to, there will always be some experiences and contexts and phenomena that you—with the particular kinds of "outsider-ness" that you bring— should step away from. Precisely to be ethical, responsible, humble, and respectful.

Listen to your internal compass.
Be honest.
Some stories might never be yours to tell.
And that's okay.

DOI: 10.4324/9781032688749-13

Index

For Product Safety Concerns and Information please contact our EU
representative GPSR@taylorandfrancis.com
Taylor & Francis Verlag GmbH, Kaufingerstraße 24, 80331 München, Germany